NORSE MYTHOLOGY

JAYDEN K. HELMAN

TABLE OF CONTENTS

INTRODUCTION

The Old Norse Religion is not that old. It is currently one of the most well-known non-monotheistic religions. It is also regarded as one of the essential mythologies for comparative research of Indo-European mythologies. This is due to the massive amount of surviving material that exists and the fact that Norse mythology remains the best documented of all the Germanic mythologies and religions.

Norse magic is hugely influenced by the concept of fate, whether concerning a person's specific destiny or affecting it. Its practitioners view it as a way to examine and perhaps exert some control over one's fate, but it is not used to change it. Seidr is most closely aligned with this idea, as in the concept of summoning power from other spiritual beings.

And, whether through written symbols or chanted words that represent those symbols, Norse magic is also devoted to the idea of being able to manifest one's desires. This manifestation process is related primarily to the practice of galdr. Runes are the key to the practice of galdr.

Once you learn how mysterious Norse magic is, it should come as no surprise that the word rune itself means mystery, whisper, or secret. We'll delve into what runes are, their meaning, and their use in magic and rituals throughout this book, and we'll also examine the alphabet of rune symbols.

The Norse gods are such entities, and they can be used for spellcasting through rune magic. There are some special requirements that the Norse gods must have to do their job, like an Icelandic runestone and a human sacrifice. But beyond these items, the only other requirement is a secret name of power.

One cannot deny that the world we call home is a highly diverse place. There are so many different cultures with their own folklore and beliefs that helped shape their religions and their history. Above all, they aided in making sense of a world in which science and information weren't readily available at all times.

The term "Old Norse religion" is the most common name assigned to the pre-Christian religious system throughout Scandinavia, with terms including, but not limited to Old Norse Paganism, Odinism, Northern Heathenism, and North Germanic Paganism. It branched out from the Germanic religion that could be encountered across Europe wherever people spoke Germanic languages.

The little things we know about Old Norse religious practice include the fact that Norse chieftains also served as spiritual leaders or priests and that horse sacrifices were a part of pagan worship practices. However, not much more is known, although scholars have managed to reconstruct a few aspects of what Old Norse worship entailed. This is based on archaeological findings, toponymy, historical linguistics, and runic inscriptions.

It is believed that Old Norse pagans focused more on rituals and worship than on belief. Rituals would take place in specific nature sites, like groves or lakes. There is evidence that houses could also be used for rituals, some of which were specifically built for cultic reasons.

The religion also featured shamans who practiced a kind of sorcery called Seiðr. Seiðr is thought to have been connected to both the shaping and the telling of the future. A variety of burial rites were also included in the Old Norse worship. The most known are ship burials and cremation accompanied by the deceased's personal items. However, simple burials were also a part of these rites, even if they weren't quite so common as the other forms.

Even though there is a severe lack of information on the worshiping practices, the little information on Norse mythology that survived is quite impressive. Norse mythology, which basically serves as the lore and tradition of Norse Paganism, is vast and colorful. It's full of diverse races like dwarfs, elves, spirits, and giants that dwelled in several different realms.

The advent of Christianity undoubtedly limited the amount of knowledge we could have had on Old Norse faith and practices. No matter how rich the surviving Norse texts and myths are, they were still recorded under Christian rule and transcribed by Christian scholars.

This book was written for people who want to get a better and more comprehensive understanding of the Norse religion. It covers everything from how it started right up to current times.

It also covers how to begin practicing on your own, the kinds of paths you can follow, and how to reach out to other Norse heathens and like-minded individuals.

This work aims to deepen your understanding of this wonderful and charming religion. Norse magic in your life can take many forms. It might be as simple as casting a simple spell, or it could be a complex ritual of runes and pagan beliefs. One thing is for sure, though—magic gives your life and soul purpose and substance.

If you are a beginner and just stepping into the Norse mythology domain, this book will help you examine its complex nature and present it in the simplest manner. It is a great stepping stone to explore more and delve deeper once you fathom the roots. The diversity and individuality of the Norse deities and other characters add an interesting edge to the entire narrative. This juxtaposition further enhances the way different versions of the same Norse stories are told. Some Norse men also individually worshipped certain deities which were not well-known and were less venerated during that era.

If you are already intrigued and cannot wait to discover the enchanting mythical world that led people into Norse Paganism, turn the page and get started.

CHAPTER 1

The Beginning and Explanation What Is Norse Mythology, a Brief History of the Norseman

Norse culture is famously shrouded in mystery, where loose ends lay everywhere and the archeological world is beyond curious in finding the truth behind their daily and religious practices. There must be a distinct understanding of what it meant to be a Norseman and what other civilizations influenced and molded their culture. They existed as a group of people settling from their migrations as Germanic tribes up into the creeks and mountains of Scandinavia.

Let us take you back in time for a minute. The era is roughly between 500 and 800 C.E., called the Scandinavian Iron Age, and Roman influences are leaving a mark on these Scandinavian tribes that had migrated north from Germanic regions. The trading, warring, and interaction with these Romans passed on the beliefs and myths of their Roman pantheon onto the Northmen, thus evolving over the centuries into the Norse gods we know today.

Then, between 800 and 1100 C.E., the Viking Age was in full throttle. Ships were built, warriors were made, trades were finalized, and slaves were sold. The seas were the roads to new worlds, to riches, to new languages, and to a new god. Christian influence started taking hold both within Scandinavian kingdoms, introducing politics and economy, and within the many Viking settlements, it also affected social and religious life.

The truth is that Norse history is a Sudoku puzzle. Bits and pieces try to fit into place in historians' minds, but it's almost impossible due to our obvious lack of context. That makes the incredible mystery even more intriguing as there is so much more to learn and discover each time!

Norsemen is a term used for the Nordic people who lived in the North Atlantic region of what we know today as Scandinavia (Norway, Denmark, Sweden, and later, Iceland). An Old Norse language was established based on Germanic and Indo-European origins before the Viking Age. Although basic agriculture collapsed by 550 C.E. and was only restored towards the 8th century, historical evidence begins to show us a more detailed picture of set practices and beliefs coinciding with foreign influences. A more controlled paganism, if you will.

Their early society was not technically a literary one, and looking into their lives requires an understanding of their oral tradition, seen in early rune inscriptions and later in the sagas and poems. The stories were told, but the reasons and methods were left for interpretation.

The Norse were predominantly farmers, fishermen, and traders. It is often overlooked that their lifestyles were more than just pillaging and conquering. Their connection with their mythologies and their rituals of magic is rooted heavily in their actual day-to-day lives, rather than it being, for instance, a civilization polarized by different beliefs. They were unified and complex.

The Norsemen, as we call them today, were not connected to the name or function of Viking when at home in their Nordic countries. If you had to be in that time, Norse or Viking would not be a word you understood or conceptualized the way we do in the modern world. You were a part of a people who lived simply in the Scandinavian wilderness and who hunted, farmed, fished, cultivated livestock, spoke to the gods, and, at times, partook in a civil war among neighboring villages and clans. Positions of the hierarchy were established and overthrown many times, and slaves were commonplace. Kings and magnates (chieftains) were quite literally the men who owned the biggest farm or the most ships. Each clan or merchant town stood independent from the other and later, with social evolution, regions and kingdoms were formed.

A simple subsistence level of farm work and living in rural farmsteads was a picture of normal Norse life. Villages usually consisted of between 15 and 60 people depending on their location for trade and agriculture.

Throughout the Viking Age, social structures began to evolve and encompass three main tiers:

- The elite, who were the wealthiest families like kings or chieftains.
- The free men and women. Here we see the majority of the population who might have owned their own land, worked the farm or traded goods and slaves.
- Slaves were known as thralls. Before slavery ended towards the late Middle Ages, the purchase and sale of human lives were considered standard practice.

Mortality rates were also very high and it is said that around 30–40% of children died before adulthood due to famine and diseases. We could see why the Vikings decided to venture to new lands, as theirs was hostile and unforgiving, especially in winter.

The trade routes of spices, silk, pottery, and silver were established and became a vital source of income as well as the trade of knowledge and information.

Curious by nature and strong by breeding, these people were tenacious and courageous, capable of feats that later civilizations would never reach. A mixture of magic and hard reality was what they lived and abided by—basic rules of engagement both with their peers and with the spirit world.

Many historians turn to the belief that Viking raids were assembled first and foremost to enslave the local people and take them back to their country to make use of or trade with. Mainly women were captured, but men and children were also taken. The slave trade focused on the continent of Britain but also extended across the Mediterranean from Spain to Egypt.

The evidence seen besides oral accounts is in the finding of collars and shackles around the ancient urban centers. Slaves were used for many activities such as textile manufacturing, ship building, farming, and most of the unpleasant jobs done around the homestead. Sexual slavery as well as intermarriage was another reason the Vikings traded so loosely with the slave women and children of England and France.

As the Norse had a very patriotic culture, most women stayed in the villages while the men went on their raids or fishing trips. Some women did join in sailing to other lands to settle with their families and some did really train as shield maidens and joined the men in battle. We speak of the free women who were wives, sisters, and daughters. Slave women were nowhere near treated the same.

The women had a strong standing when it came to matters of healing, magic, and rituals. This book is centered on magic and ritualism, and women played a central part in that field.

Within the threshold of the home, women were in charge of preparing food, cleaning the house, purchasing and repairing clothing items, baking, cooking, preparing alcoholic drinks, and making dairy products. The men hunted and maintained their agriculture and livestock farming, though both women and men took the role of shepherd. In summer months, when the work was plenty, usually the whole household pulled their weight and assisted in the sowing and reaping.

Women did have a voice in gatherings and meetings, and were able to divorce their men if they chose. Such an oddity if you think how other civilizations operating at the time still held a very backward view of marriage and fidelity. This is not to say that men were faithful in the way we know fidelity today.

Normally unions and weddings were arranged by the patriarch of the family, both for social uplifting and monetary gain, but seen too were relationships based on love and companionship.

How the Cosmos was Created

The Norse cosmogony is probably one of the more extensive in all of literature.

According to Gylfaginning by Snorri Sturluson, the dawn of the cosmos begins with a gaping void called Ginnungagap (Old Norse for "gaping abyss" or "yawning void"). Ginnungagap was there before anything green ever existed in the world, laying between the realm of fire, Muspelheim. That was controlled by a fire giant named Surtr, and the realm of ice, Niflheim. This was the home of Hvergelmir, the well from which all the rivers flow, and also home to the glacial rivers of Élivágar.

While Ginnungagap enveloped darkness and quiet, massive flames from Muspelheim and staggering frost from Niflheim began creeping towards each other until they collided in Ginnungagap.

In the middle of the sizzling and hissing of such a union, the ice melted because of the fire, and sparks began to sputter out. The sparks went on to create the stars, the Sun, and the Moon, and the water drops from the melted ice, formed into a being called Ymir ("Screamer"), the first of the very powerful and very destructive giants. Ymir was described as being hermaphrodite and also that he could asexually reproduce.

Ymir

More and more giants leaped off from his body while he was asleep, springing up from his sweat and his legs.

The frost of Niflheim continued to melt, and soon a cow named Audhumla emerged from the ice. She helped nourish Ymir with her milk, and in return, she was nourished by salt-licks in the ice. Audhumla's licks gradually weathered the ice and helped uncover Buri (which means 'The Progenitor'), who was the first ancestor of the Æsir.

Buri proceeded to have a son who was named Bor (Meaning 'Son'). Bor then married Bestla (possibly meaning 'wife'), who was the daughter of the giant named Bolthorn ('meaning 'Baleful Thorn']). Bor and Bestla had three children who were half-giants, half-gods. Those children were Óðinn, Vili, and Vé, the first Æsir.

However, the brothers decided to slay Ymir and use his vast body to build the world. His blood became the world's oceans, his skin and muscles became the soil, and his hair became flora. They turned his brains into clouds and formed the sky from his skull, held high above the Earth by a dwarf placed in each of the four cardinal directions.

Eventually, Óðinn, Vili, and Vé created the first people from two tree trunks and fenced them in what would become the human realm, Midgard, to keep them safe from the giants. The first humans were Ask and Embla.

The Norse believed that the world was separated into nine interconnected realms. Some of those realms received extensive attention in the lore, with the primary focus on Asgard and Vanaheim, the home realms of the Æsir and the Vanir, respectively. Midgard, the mortals' home realm, and Niflheim featured in the creation myth and later became the home realm of Hel, the underworld queen.

These realms were all supported by Yggdrasil, with Asgard high on the tree's canopy, Midgard in the middle (hence the name), surrounded by an impenetrable sea, and then finally the underworld Niflheim deep down among Yggdrasil's roots.

The Many Races of the Norse Mythos

The Æsir

The Æsir are the main pantheon in the Norse faith. They were later united with the second pantheon, the Vanir.

The Æsir war with the Vanir has caused a rather important amount of theorizing and speculation among scholars. While other polytheistic religions often have varying groups of gods that wage war against each other, they usually differ in age, with one group being the elder and another the younger. The Æsir and the Vanir, however, appear to be contemporaries.

The first Æsir were Vili, Vé, and Óðinn, which are all names that come from words meant to refer to distinct mental or spiritual states. Vili to conscious desire or will, vé to the spiritual and the sacred, and finally óðr to the ecstatic or manic.

In both of the Eddas, the word Æsir is used for the male gods, while the term used for the goddesses is Asynjur.

Many of the Æsir origins remain unexplained since the sources have been lost. There is only mention of how Óðinn and his brothers were created. However, there is no mention of Heimdallr's or Ullr's connection.

Óðinn's children with giantesses are also considered Æsir.

The Vanir

The second pantheon is the Vanir. The Vanir consists of the god Njǫrðr along with his children, gods Freyja and Freyr. These three are the most important Vanir who join the Æsir after being taken hostages following a war between the two pantheons. The Vanir were primarily connected to fertility and cultivation, while the Æsir were mostly associated with war and power.

The Jötnar

The Jötnar (singular Jötunn) is a race that acts as a foil to the races of Order in the Norse mythos. Other terms can be used to refer to them, such as giants, trolls, risi, or thurs and mostly live in the Jötunheimr realm, although they can live in other places.

The term giant sometimes is used interchangeably with the word Jötunn. However, the Jötnar are not automatically remarkably large. They can be described as either extremely beautiful or exceedingly grotesque.

Despite their antagonistic role in the Mythos, several deities are described as members of the Jötnar, such as Gerðr and Skaði, who are married to Freyr and Njǫrðr respectively.

Skaði, in particular, has evidently been worshipped by the Old Norse pagans, as evident by references in Lokasenna and in toponyms, like the Swedish Skedevi.

Not only that but there are many of the Æsir that are descended from Jötnar, Óðinn, and Thórr included. This suggests that the divide distinction between the Æsir and the Jötnar is not as distinct as modern people believe.

In actuality, the main difference between the Æsir, the Vanir, and the Jötnar, seems to be their domains. The Æsir domains revolve around war and conquests, the Vanir are all about fertility, well-being, exploration, and wealth, and the Jötnar are a wise but malevolent and chaotic race.

The Elves and Dwarves

The Ljósálfar (Light elves) and the Dökkálfar/svartálfar (Dark elves/Black elves) are two separate races of elves that live in the Nine Realms. The Ljósálfar are "fairer than the sun" and dwell in Álfheimr, while the Dökkálfar lives in the earth and are dark as pitch and very different in disposition than their light cousins. The dark elves may even be the Dwarves of the Cosmos.

The Norns

The Nornir (Norse singular: Norn) is a trio of deities that measure and control the fate of all beings in the cosmos, deities and mortals alike. They were named Urðr, Verðandi, Skuld. Urðr 's name is like the past tense of the verb verða, which means "to become," which possibly means "Became," thus representing the past. Verðandi, on the other hand, is the present participle of the verb verða, which would be "Becoming," representing the present. Skuld comes from the modal skulu, which means "shall," representing the future.

According to the surviving lore, the Norns live under the roots of Yggdrasill. There, they weave the tapestry of fate, with each life represented by a string on their loom.

Dagr and Nótt

Dagr (Old Norse for "Day") is the personified deity of the day. He is the son of the god Dellingr and is connected to the bright horse Skinfaxi, who draws the day to mortals. His mother is either by the personified Night, Nótt, or the personified earth Jörð.

Nótt (Old Norse for "Night") is the personified deity of the night. She is the daughter of Nörvi and is connected to the horse Hrímfaxi. She was married three times. The third time it was to the god Dellingr and resulted in the birth of Dagr. She is also Thórr's grandmother.

Máni and Sól

Máni and Sól (which is Old Norse for "Moon" and "Sun" respectively) are the sibling personifications of the moon and the sun in several Germanic mythologies. According to both the Eddas, they are children of Mundilfari.

According to Sturluson, Máni is followed by two children named Hjúki and Bil through the sky.

Sól can also be called Sunna, or sometimes as Álfröðull and drives the sun horse carriage across the sky. She is foretold to be slain by a monstrous wolf during Ragnarök. However, before that, she will have born a daughter who will take over her mother's course through the sky.

She is married to Glenr (Old Norse for "opening in the clouds").

Yggdrasil and its Residents

The top of Yggdrasil was said to reach far into the sky. The sacred European Ash tree was supported by three roots that stretched all the way to the spring of Hvergelmir, the well of Urðarbrunnr, and the well of Mímisbrunnr.

The Norns, who were female beings that spun the threads of fate, would draw water from Urðarbrunnr and use it to water Yggdrasil.

Four stars, named Dáinn, Duneyrr, Dvalinn, and Duraþrór, would constantly feed on Yggdrasil. However, the tree's vitality persisted, and it remained evergreen.

On the uppermost branch sat an unnamed eagle, whose wings' beating caused the winds in Midgard.

The great serpent Niðhǫggr, dwelled at the roots of Yggdrasil, constantly gnawing at them. The rude messenger squirrel Ratatoskr journeyed back and forth the tree carrying messages and insults.

The nine realms around Yggdrasil were often mentioned in the Old Norse sources that existed throughout history, but they were never clearly listed. However, some scholars have suggested identification and theories, although interpretation varies from one writer to another in later texts.

The nine realms are most commonly accepted to be Ásgarðr, Vanaheimr, Álfheimr, Miðgarðr, Jötunheimr, Múspellsheimr, Svartálfaheimr, Niflheimr (which is often correlated with Hel), and possibly Niðavellir.

Asgardians

After shaping Midgard for mortals, the gods made a splendid city for themselves and named it Asgard. It was bound to the earth by the fiery bridge called Bifrost, the rainbow; the gods hoped that the giants would be unable to cross this bridge and attack them. Living humans could not pass that way either. But warriors who died bravely in battle were taken up by the Valkyries, the fierce and beautiful daughters of Odin, to Asgard. Half of them went to Odin's castle called Valhalla, where they spent their days fighting each other (not in hostility, but for practice and for the joy of battle; every evening the injured were restored to perfect health) and their nights in feasting. The other half went to Folkvangr, the great hall of Odin's wife Frigg. Frigg was the wisest of the goddesses. She watched over and had the power to alter the magical weaving which determined the fates of mortals. Sometimes, unlike her husband, she took brave women as well as brave men into her hall.

All the buildings of Asgard were made of gold. Splendor was everywhere. So were endless life and unwithering strength, thanks to the goddess Iduna's apple tree whose fruit made the eater immortal. And in one place there was something rarer than splendor or immortality—peace. That was in Breiddablik, the Peace Stead, the palace of Balder. Balder was so beautiful that he shed light where he walked, and his judgments were so wise and just that his quarrelsome fellow gods did not find fault with them.

In the midst of all this beauty, Odin was uneasy. He remembered the anger of the giants, and he feared that they would destroy everything he and his brothers and sisters had created. The warriors in Valhalla fought each other daily so that they would be a formidable force whenever the day of reckoning came, but he didn't trust that army to save him from the forces the giants could raise. He often went to his other castle Valaskjalf, whose topmost tower was so high that he could see any place in the Worlds from it; he sat alone there, looking, pondering, worrying.

But the first threat to Asgard came, not from the giants, but from another race of gods, the Vanir. Nobody remembers where they came from; perhaps they were descended from Buri or Borr's other children. Be that as it may, the Aesir (Asgard's inhabitants) and the Vanir saw each other's power from afar off, felt threatened, and attacked each other. The fighting was long and equally matched; the Vanir threw down the walls of Asgard, but they could not drive the Aesir out. Finally, weary of war and each impressed by the courage and strength of the others, they decided to make a treaty of peace. The Vanir withdrew to their own lands. Two of the Aesir went with them as hostages or ambassadors, and they soon passed out of the stories of the North. Three of the Vanir remained as hostages in Asgard: Njord, god of the sea and sailors, his son Frey, and his daughter Freya. Now Freya was a wise woman, skilled in seeing the future, and she had a set of falcon feathers that allowed the wearer to take bird shape and fly. She was also devastatingly beautiful and free with her favors to any god who struck her fancy.

The Aesir were very pleased with their hostages but less pleased with their ruined walls. Then a stranger arrived at the gates of Asgard, offering to build a better defensive wall that could withstand any assault, and promising to have the work done within a year and a half. The offer seemed good to Odin— until he heard the price. The builder demanded in payment the sun, the moon, and marriage to Freya, who was quite unwilling to be married off. The rest of the gods and goddesses didn't want to see their city stripped of light and loveliness. But Odin feared an attack that would destroy that beauty forever.

After a long argument, the gods decided to accept the builder's offer, and his price, with one condition: that the builder work alone, that the wall is completed within one winter, and that the builder agrees to go unpaid if the work wasn't finished on time. Surely, they thought, the builder couldn't work so fast— but in pride and foolishness, he might overestimate his own capabilities, and so give them most of a wall free of charge. The gods rejoiced when the builder accepted the offer, and they willingly accepted his own condition—that his stallion Svadilfari should be allowed to help him haul stone for the wall. They swore all the oaths he asked of them, pledging to give him his price if he succeeded, and pledging that no god would hurt him while he worked on the wall. (This last promise was needed because of Odin's son Thor, the strongest and shortest-tempered of the gods. No one and nothing could stand against the terrible blows of Thor's thunder-hammer Mjöllnir, and Thor's power had not taught him anything about self-restraint. But even to Thor, an oath was an oath and could not be broken.)

But what a horse Svadilfari was! His speed, his strength, the stones he could move! He worked tirelessly, day and night, and three days before winter's end the building was done except for the gate. The wall was so high and strong that the gods couldn't pretend to be dissatisfied, and the work had gone so quickly that the gods never doubted it would be finished in time. They came together to debate the only question that remained: Which of them had had the terrible idea of accepting the builder's offer? They blamed the usual suspect in such cases: Loki.

Now Loki, the son of a giant, was perhaps the cleverest of the gods, though certainly not the wisest; he was full of ingenious ideas, and seldom took thought for their long-term consequences. He didn't deny that he'd made the suggestion, which had seemed brilliant to everyone else at the time. When they seized him and threatened him with torture and death if his suggestion led to their losing Freya and the light, he was terrified and swore to them that he would make sure the builder didn't complete the work. They let him go, trusting his oath to hold him, and also knowing that without his help they could see no way out of the bad bargain.

That night the builder went into the forest with his stallion to haul stone. He gloated in his heart, thinking of Freya, and also thinking of the rage and humiliation of the gods. He didn't notice the first time the mare whinnied in the depths of the wood. He didn't catch her scent in the wind. But Svadilfari did. He neighed, tossed his head, tore the lead from his master's hands, and galloped into the darkness, chasing the mare who fled before him swiftly and silent as a shadow. The builder gave chase, shouting and cursing, but the horses left him far behind.

The builder, for all his strength and skill, couldn't carry the stone by himself. On the last day of winter, the gods pointed out that his work was unfinished, and he'd have to take himself off without pay. His fury was so fierce that it shattered his disguise, and he stood before them in his own form—a frost-giant, eager to harm the gods who had destroyed Ymir. Thor, seeing that, pulled out the thunder-hammer and struck the builder a blow that shattered him.

So the wall was built, and the gods kept Freya and the sun and moon. But the story of how the gods had cheated the giant spread far and wide, and it only deepened the hatred of the other frost-giants and their determination to take revenge. While the rest of the gods feasted and celebrated, Odin brooded about how and when that revenge would come.

But Loki, eleven months later, took a mare's shape again and gave birth to a fine strong foal, Svadilfari's son. The foal was a marvel, eight-legged and wonderfully strong and fast, and Odin rode him on his longest journeys.

Status of Norse Mythology

Norse and Germanic mythology heavily influenced the naming of the days of the week. Sunday, for example, is named after Sol, the sun goddess. Her two magnificent horses drag her across the globe. They are pursued by the enormous wolf Skoll, who snaps at her ankles every now and again, causing a solar eclipse.

Mani, her brother, is the inspiration for Monday. Hati, the enormous wolf, is pursuing his horse-drawn chariot. A moon eclipse occurs just as he is about to catch up.

Tuesday is named after Tyr, the god of war and justice, a difficult portfolio to balance, even then.

Wednesday is named after Odin since his name in Old English was Woden.

Thursday is named after Thor, the god of thunder.

Friday is Frigga's Day, for the wife of Odin. Frigga was a complex goddess, as she knew the fate of everyone, even after Ragnarök, but she never revealed it. The day is also connected with the Roman pantheon's goddess Venus, Frigga's cognate.

Saturday was named for the planet Saturn. In Roman mythology, Saturn was the god of agriculture. In the Norse pantheon, there isn't a direct correlation as many of the gods and goddesses are associated with fertility, farming, and harvesting, so it is the only name for a day of the week that does not have a particularly Norse connection.

Many social traditions, especially around Christian religious events, hearken back to Norse mythology: Yule logs, Christmas trees, and decorating eggs at Easter time are only a few. Perhaps Santa Claus driving his reindeer through the sky is an echo of the Wild Hunt. One story mentions the tradition of leaving a sack of hay out for Sleipnir during this time. Perhaps this evolved into leaving a plate of cookies and milk or beer for Santa?

The influence of Norse mythology is even more visible today in a revival of interest in heathenry, particularly in Scandinavia, Iceland, and the United States of America. This revival has "the aim of forming a faith tradition that is deeply rooted in the ancient past and yet can speak to the needs and concerns of modern people" (Grundy, 2015). This interest has taken various forms.

Theodism is a religious movement started in 1976 by Garman Lord. He looks for historical accuracy in how he follows the old gods. This is not a matter of simply duplicating rituals but of truly contextualizing ancient teachings and applying the principles to the modern world. The concept of tribalism and hierarchy is an essential part of re-developing this way of living. Wiccan beliefs are more rooted in Celtic than Germanic paganism, but there are similarities in the strong influence of the belief in gods and goddesses, and in nature worship. Its practice involves manipulating nature through various rituals in attempts to gain power, prestige, love, or whatever else a Wiccan wants.

Ásatrú is probably the most important modern pagan religion today. The word means "belief in the gods," and as a religion, it has been expanding steadily in the United Kingdom, France,

USA, South Africa, Europe, and Scandinavia. We introduced Sveinbjörn Beinteinsson (1924–1993) earlier; he was a sheep farmer who formally founded Ásatrú in Iceland. In 1945, he published a book of Icelandic rhymed poetry. He had a wonderfully resonant voice and the physical appearance of an ancient Skald. He made regular public appearances reading his poems and reciting the sagas from the Eddas. He has also made many recordings, some of which can be found on the internet today. His petition to the Icelandic government led to Ásatrú's recognition as an Icelandic, neopagan congregation of faith, reviving the pre-Christian religion of Scandinavia. It was officially recognized as a national religion in 1973 in Iceland followed shortly by recognition in Denmark and Norway.

The present (priest) is Hilmar Örn Hilmarsson. In 2015, the members opened the very first modern temple to the Norse gods. It is located in Thingvellir National Park, near Reykjavik. Ásatrú communities are called Kindreds, and the meetings are called Blots which means sacrifice. Mead, a honeyed wine, beer, or cider, is consecrated to a particular god and, after everyone has taken a drink, the rest is poured out as a libation to that god. One variation of this ritual is a Sumbel which is a toast in three rounds. The first toast is to Odin, the second toast is to the ancestors and the honorable dead, and the third toast is open to anyone.

The followers are committed to the Nine Noble Qualities: honor, fidelity, courage, truth, discipline, industriousness, self-reliance, hospitality, and perseverance. One should live one's life with due regard to these virtues and, if you succeed, you will go on in the afterlife to "greater fulfillment, pleasure, and challenge." If one lives badly, you will be "separated from your kin and live-in dullness and gloom" in your afterlife. The movement is growing steadily and earning more official recognition every day. Recently, the U.S. Army and Air Force have added Heathen and Ásatrú to the religious preferences list their recruits must fill to describe their religion.

The Odin Brotherhood is a version of Ásatrú, and they call themselves a secret society for men and women who value knowledge, freedom, and power.

Norse Mythology God/Goddess of Magic

Like the Greeks and their Titans, the Norse have a unique name for their primordial gods; today, referred to as "giants," the more appropriate term might be "devourers." And like the Greeks and their Olympian gods, a younger group (Aesir gods) overthrew the older, coarser giants.

Vanir Gods and Goddesses

These gods usually lived in Vanaheim or called it their place of origin.

Njörd

Father of Freyr and Freya. Njörd's wife was one of the giants named Skadi. His responsibilities included the sea and fertility.

Freyr (also Frey)

An honorary member of the Aesir, originally of the Vanir. He was the god of sexual and agricultural fertility. He was frequently accompanied by his great boar, Gullinborsti ("Golden Bristled"). Though originally from Vanaheim, and a member of Asgard, his home was in Alfheim—land of the elves. A great deal of speculation has surrounded Freyr on this point of fact. Was he their king? An ally? The original texts never clarify this issue. Understandably, Freyr has slept with a great many goddesses and female giants. He had even slept with his sister, Freya. Incest was taboo amongst the Germanic peoples, but not amongst the Vanir.

Freya (also Freyja)

Like her brother, Freyr, she was an honorary member of the Aesir. Her husband's name was Odr. Because of the similarity in husband and wife names, a strong case has been made that Odr is none other than Odin and that Freya is merely another name of Frigg, Odin's wife. Loki had accused her of having slept with all the gods, including her brother and even some elves. She is a goddess of fertility, love, beauty, and elegant property. If she had lived today, she might even be called the "party girl" of the gods. She wielded great power—the seidhr—manipulating the prosperity, health, and desires of others. Amongst her many powers is the ability to shapeshift into the form of a falcon.

Nanna

In some versions, she was the wife of the Aesir god, Baldr; in others, she spurned Baldr and married the human named Hoder. In the text of Gesta Danorum, Nanna was merely the mortal daughter of King Gevar. However, in Snorri Sturluson's writings, she was the daughter of Nepr, one of Odin's sons. So, this would make her Odin's granddaughter and Baldr's niece. In such a case, she would be pure Aesir and not Vanir. And as Baldr's wife and niece, incest would also be a part of the behavior in Asgard. Like so many myths of the ancient past, conflicting versions make it difficult to keep the gods and goddesses straight.

Hoenir

Originally, he was an Aesir god, but after the truce of the Aesir-Vanir war, he was given to the Vanir as a hostage. The few stories about him seem to portray him as a bumbling idiot. When the Vanir consulted him, Hoenir would always get his answers from the giant, Mímir, a source of great wisdom. When Mímir was unavailable, Hoenir would merely mumble some ambiguous reply.

In Prose Edda, Hoenir is ironically mentioned as the source of humanity's ability to reason. In another work, the Gylfaginning, humanity's sources of reason are Vili and Vé, Odin's two brothers. Could Hoenir merely have been another name for one of Odin's brothers? According to another source, the Voluspa, Hoenir would be one of the few gods to survive Ragnarök—the end of their current world and the beginning of the next.

Aesir Gods and Asynjur Goddesses

Aesir is more properly the male term for the gods of Asgard, and Asynjur is the female term. For our convenience, we will refer to both as Aesir. The following gods called Asgard "home":

Odin

He was king of the gods, a position held in other pantheons by the likes of Zeus and Jupiter.

Frigg

She was the wife of Odin. As we've already seen, she may well be from Vanaheim, originally known by Freya.

Thor

He was one of the sons of Odin. This was the god of thunder and storms and a fierce warrior who carried a hammer called Mjolnir, fashioned for him by the dwarves.

Loki

An adopted giant of Jötnar, son of Odin. He was a trickster, frequently causing trouble in Asgard and elsewhere.

Heimdall

This god could see and hear with such clarity, Odin sent him to guard the entrance to Asgard—where the great rainbow bridge, called the Bifrost, connected the home of the gods with the rest of the universe. He was said to have had nine mothers. He required far less rest than even a bird, so he rarely needed to leave his post. He could see for hundreds of kilometers during light and dark. And he could hear the grass grow. Asgard's enemies had little chance to slip past this god unnoticed.

Ullr

Was the son of the goddess Sif. He excelled in hunting, skating, skiing, and archery. According to Saxo Grammaticus, a Danish historian of the Middle Ages, Ullr took leadership over the gods when Odin had been in exile. His name made its appearance in some solemn oaths, such as swearing by the "ring of Ullr," or the time when Odin swore the blessings of "Ullr and all the gods" to the person who might rescue him from between two fires.

Sif

Goddess of grain and wife of Thor. She was also the mother of

Ullr, but it seemed the father was someone other than Thor, perhaps before Thor and Sif became husband and wife.

Bragi

This god was the official poet and minstrel of the Asgard court.

Idun

She was the wife of Bragi. This goddess dispensed a magical fruit that gave the gods their long life.

Baldr

A son of Odin and Frigg. In some versions, he was considered to be radiant and beloved by all the Aesir gods.

Hödr

His name meant simply "warrior," and there was not much mentioned about him except the one who had killed Baldr.

Forseti

His name meant "chairman." He was not mentioned very much in the old texts. One poem of the Poetic Edda mentioned that he settled disputes. In the Prose Edda, Sturluson told us that Forseti was the son of Baldr and Nanna, a claim that at least one scholar disputes.

Vili and Vé

Two brothers of Odin, who helped slay the giant, Ymir, and form the world with the giant's body. When Odin was on his many travels searching for wisdom, Frigg (Freya?) would grow lonely. So, one or the other of the brothers would keep her company, even at night.

Tyr

In the literature, he was a minor god, and little was said about him. But there are so many strong references to him that it seems likely that the Viking Age believers had merely forgotten Tyr in favor of Odin. For instance, only Tyr was brave enough to risk his hand in the mouth of Fenrir to bind him with a magic cord.

The Jötnar Giants and Cohorts

Jötnar is the plural form of jötunn—the giants of Jötunheim. The giants were frequently enemies of the humans and the Aesir gods. Though they are frequently referred to as giants in the literature, the original meaning of these creatures was "devourers."

Fenrir

A giant wolf and son of Loki and giantess Angrboda. He was the brother of Hel and Jormungand.

Hel

She was the goddess of Helheim—the underworld where the dead were kept. She was the daughter of Loki and Angrboda and thus the sister of Fenrir and Jormungand. Her name meant "hidden."

Jormungand

A giant serpent and son of Loki and giantess Angrboda. Accordingly, he was the brother of Fenrir and Hel. He circled the earth in the oceans of Midgard. He is frequently called the Midgard Serpent. His name means "great beast." He and Thor were destined to slay each other in Ragnarök.

Skadi

A giantess who loved the mountains where the snow never melts. She was considered to have been a great huntress with a bow and snowshoes. She had been married to the Vanir god, Njörd, with whom she produced two children—Freyr and Freya. And if Freya was another name for Frigg, then Skadi was the grandmother of Baldr.

Surt

His name meant "black" in Old Norse. He was a fire giant who spent a great deal of time in Muspelheim—the realm of fire. His favorite weapon was a burning sword.

Nidhogg

One of the preeminent serpents beneath the Yggdrasil world tree. There, he, and his fellow dragons would eat at the roots of the tree, causing great damage. This threatened all Nine Realms. His name meant "he who strikes with malice." Though he did not live in Jötunheim, he is certainly associated with their efforts to pull the cosmos back into chaos.

Skoll and Hati

Two wolves that forever chased the Sun and the Moon to devour them.

Aegir and Ran

These two were husband and wife, respectively. They lived in a great hall underneath the ocean. Aegir's name meant "ocean," while his wife's name meant "robber." Aegir was usually shown as a friendly host. His wife, however, was frequently seen drowning luckless sailors and pulling them down to her underwater world. The couple had nine daughters. Of all the giants, these two seemed to have the friendliest relationship with the Aesir gods, quite often inviting them to feast with them.

Garm

A great wolf who fought the god Tyr during Ragnarök. There is some evidence that Garm is merely another name for Fenrir.

Trolls, Dwarves, Elves, and Giants

Trolls

Some tales from Sweden describe trolls as monstrous beings with many heads who can either live in the forest and mountains or in caves. The first kind of trolls that live in the mountains are known to be large, aggressive, stupid, and slow beings, always getting outwitted by the hero in the story. Those that live in caves are shy and seen as shorter than humans with stumpy arms and legs but with a fair amount of intelligence. They use the environment around them to influence their power or protect themselves and hide. These creatures emerged into mythology from the idea of the giants (jötun) in their cosmology and realms, as the word troll in Old Norse is jätte.

Dwarves

The dwarves were known to be crafty beings that live in the realm of Midgard, hidden from humans in subterranean realms. The tales of dwarves go far back into mythology and creation, as they were known to be born of the flesh of the giant Ymir, along with the rest of their cosmos. They were molded by the Æsir into figures that resemble humans, but much shorter and gifted with intelligence and skill. These beings are artists in creating all sorts of things from jewelry to weapons and other intricate pieces. We see their skill in the creation of Thor's hammer Mjölnir crafted by the dwarves Brokkr and Eitri, as well as many other weapons in the gods' possession.

The Elves

The Vanir seemed to have a particular bond with the elves who were described as being light and made of light. Freyr, a Vanir god, was noted as being the lord of the elven homeworld Alfheim. With the Vanir gods being associated with harvest, nature, and fertility, it is no stretch to assume the elves shared these characteristics.

Humans and elves had a strange relationship according to myth, with the elves both causing and healing diseases among the humans, and instances of interbreeding were strongly hinted at. The Norse peoples were known to venerate the elves for centuries after their conversion to Christianity and the lapsing of the worship of the Norse gods.

CHAPTER 2

The Origins of the Vikings, the Start
of the Viking Era, the Other Side of
Vikings History, the Viking Life, Viking
Spirituality

The Origins of Vikings

Vikings came from Sweden, Norway, and Denmark, many hundreds of years before they were recognized as stand-alone countries, and they were mostly land-owning farmers and fishermen. They lived in villages ruled by chieftains or clan leaders, and they had few towns. Chieftains often fought for dominance over the lands, and with a seemingly inexhaustible arsenal of strong men who sought adventure, it was fairly easy for skillful leaders to organize armies and fearful bands. Historians are unsure what prompted Vikings to leave their lands and become seafaring pillagers, but they do propose a couple of theories.

The political instability caused by the frequent clashes between clans makes a good motive for branching out. Another would be localized overpopulation, which led to families owning smaller and smaller lands that could no longer provide sustenance for all the family members. Additionally, around the seventh and eighth centuries, the Vikings refined the way they constructed ships and vessels, adding sails and modifying their structures to sustain longer voyages. These longships were swift and shallow, allowing them to go across the North Sea and land on the beaches of unsuspecting lands. If we consider shipping advances, the troubled socio-economic situation of the Vikings at the time, the adventurous nature of these warrior-spirited people, and the tales of riches brought along by merchants, it's not hard to understand why one day they decided to raid the coasts of Europe.

The Start of the Viking Era

The first historical account of a Viking classical hit-and-run raid dates back to the year 793, when a monastery in Lindisfarne, England was plundered of its sacred, golden religious artifacts. Though, as a side note here, it is unlikely that this was the first time the Vikings attacked England. Evidence shows that English coastal villages had started to organize defenses against sea attacks earlier in the eighth century, suggesting that there were Viking raids or at least attempts before the attack on the Lindisfarne monastery. Many medieval English documents refer to them as "seagoing pagans" for their tendency to target holy places, which, to be fair, were full of unarmed men and gold, so who can blame the Vikings for taking the opportunity? The term "Viking," which is derived from the old Scandinavian word vikingir (pirate) or from the word vik, which means "bay," was popularized closer to the end of the historical Viking Age. Terms such as Dani (inhabitants of present Denmark), Normani (Northmen), and simply pagani (pagans) were more generally used when referring to the Scandinavian warriors by the European people who were unlucky enough to face their wrath.

From the year 793 forwards, Viking bands consisting of freemen, retainers, and young, adventure-seeking men led by chieftains had gone on to further attack England and its surroundings, especially Scotland, Ireland, and France. Additionally, some accounts from the latter years of the Viking Era speak of Viking attacks or sightings in the Iberian Peninsula, Ukraine, Russia, and even the Byzantine Empire. Originally, the raids were pretty small-scale. There were only a handful of ships, and the Vikings would happily return home when they collected enough booty or if they encountered a resilient defense. But from the 850s, the Vikings began to double down on the force and organization of their raids, establishing bases in the newly conquered lands and starting to dominate the surrounding island areas.

Vikings were those who sailed the northern Atlantic seas to run raids or settle in new lands. The word Viking is technically the verb for "making a sea voyage" in the Old Norse language, so the Norsemen would "go Viking."

The period is now 800 C.E. and the Norsemen have mastered shipbuilding in a way that allowed them to navigate rough seas as well as narrow rivers with dexterity. The people are eager and strong, ready to venture to new lands. Many warriors were sailing across the Atlantic or traveling the Mediterranean, some strategizing river access to major cities across Europe, and others accessing the far regions of the East through the Baltic channels of trade. Other Norse-Icelandic people even attempted to settle in the Americas. The headgear they wore never consisted of horned helmets, as is usually portrayed in media, but rather simple iron helmets. This misrepresentation was established through Christian-influenced literature.

The pièce de résistance was their ability to sail. Building ships that were both agile and strong, they designed them with planks that followed the tree's grain, making them naturally stronger. The clinker method, which was a pattern for building the hull with overlapping planks riveted together, was ingenious in allowing flexibility with a comparatively lightweight and shallow depth structure. This allowed smooth navigation during raids where speed and maneuverability were crucial.

With the addition of sun stones and sun charts that would track the sun's path over the sky during adverse weather, the Vikings were unstoppable.

Making use initially of water advantage, stealth, speed, and brute strength, the Vikings later evolved into a more sophisticated and political force and what some widely considered the reason the Viking Era ended.

Different Ventures

Historical resources from the first Viking raids in the late 7th century are terribly limited. What we do know is that the Norse were not strictly divided into separate states or regions as we may see now. The Anar-Ulstar Chronicles from Ireland and the Anglo-Saxon Chronicles mention that the Norwegians, Swedes, and Danish all considered themselves as different people and different groups. "The difference between these groups would have been small, if not imperceptible to our modern lens, but to the Vikings, they would have been paramount," (Adrien, 2021).

So it's safe to say that they were broadly separated into three main groups:

- The Danish Vikings were seen as the strongest of the factions, with more militaristic people and a stronger political mind. They dominated over their initial raids and settlements and conquered with more ease. Due to their affinity for political agendas, they grew faster and stronger by ensuring their confirmation to Christianity would be conducive to gaining more title and protection over land and people.

Much more is known about the Danish Vikings than their cousins, and it is believed to mainly be due to the fact that they dominated regions that had people who were better at chronologizing and depicting the battles and events of history at the time.

They were able to both outwit and outmaneuver the enemy, which consisted mainly of Britain, Normandy (a region of France), and certain parts of the Mediterranean. The Danish settled well in Normandy where native women were taken as wives which brought about more social coercion.

- The Swedish Vikings were also known as Varangians or the Rus due to their founding the regions in what is known as Russia today. They were tradesmen and explorers, rather than pillagers and murderers like their counterparts. They excelled and focused their trade on the Middle Eastern areas of the Baltic. If you look at the map of Scandinavia, you will see that Sweden's waters face more eastwards than north or west, giving them more availability and access to those lands and regions. Being merchants and mercenaries too, the Swedes took to more honest work than raiding and pillaging. Being especially proud of their heritage, they were the last of the three groups to convert to Christianity.
- With the Norwegian Vikings, we see the bravest, crazed, and barbaric warriors of their time and standing. Berserkers (Vikings who wore the pelts of wolves and bears to bring strength in battle) were found among these warriors and were the only Vikings to be known to use the ax as a weapon in battle. The Norwegians were the best shipbuilders and sailors who reached the

farthest coasts of Iceland, Greenland, and the Americas.

Vikings Spirituality

The Vikings believed in numerous gods and goddesses who were elaborately described in Norse mythology. Vikings were followers of Norse Paganism. There were little, or no written sources or codified texts representing the Old Norse religion during the Viking Age. Along with the belief in a number of gods, goddesses, and divine beings, the Vikings also practiced multiple traditional rituals and rites, especially during special occasions and events to commemorate them.

The most important deities of Norse Mythology included Thor, Odin, Heimdall, Loki, Balder, Tyr, and Frigg. Each of these divine beings was associated with certain elements or things, and each of them had unique functions and powers too. For example, Thor was the god of thunder and lightning.

Vikings believed in two tribes of gods, namely Aesir and Vanir. Odin, Thor, Frigg, Balder, Loki, and others belonged to the Aesir tribe. Odin was the chief god as well as the god of wisdom, death, war, and property. His wife was Frigg, and she was the goddess of marriage and motherhood. Thor, the most powerful among the pantheon of Viking gods, was Odin's son and the god of thunder, lightning, and storms. Loki was considered to be a powerful but unpredictable god who gave birth to many evil beings and creatures.

All the gods and goddesses played important parts and roles in Norse mythology. The various details and stories of the pantheon of gods and goddesses of Norse Paganism are contained in Norse mythology, along with creation myths and conflicts between gods and humans, gods and heroes, and many other tales. According to Norse mythology, our cosmology, consisting of many worlds and realms, is centered on Yggdrasil's cosmic tree.

Rites and Rituals

Vikings believed in and commonly practiced sacrificial rites and rituals. They sacrificed different animals like cows, roosters, hens, and dogs. Even human sacrifice, especially the slaves of Vikings, was a common occurrence in the Viking Age. Human sacrifices took place at specific religious locations and/or temples.

So why and when were sacrifices performed by the Vikings? Sacrificial rituals were performed in honor of various gods and goddesses and on special occasions. For example, sacrifices were conducted before the Viking warriors set out for battle or set out on a journey, especially sea voyages, and even after completing a deal. Also, sacrifices were typical rituals during certain ceremonies such as marriages and funerals.

Marriage Ceremonies Among the Vikings

Marriages were an important aspect of Viking culture and tradition. Often, preparations for marriages would take up to three years because the concerned families needed to settle dowries, property transfers, and inheritances through the marriage. Marriages were grandly celebrated, and festivities could go on from three to seven days.

Friday was considered an auspicious day for marriages because it honored the goddess of marriage. An important event during the marriage was the handing over of the family's sword (usually passed on for generations) by the groom to his bride. She would hold it safe until she could pass it on to their son. In return, the bride passed her father's sword to the groom as a symbol of transferring her guardianship from her father to her husband.

Role of Magic in Norse Mythology and the Viking Culture

Magic was a potent element of the Vikings' belief system. They were predisposed to different forms of superstition. The Vikings believed that Odin discovered the power and wisdom of magic. He is believed to have invoked a volva (a class of powerful Norse witches) to get some questions answered. Interestingly, Norse mythology depicts mostly feminine figures practicing magic, driving the idea that magic was a feminine prerogative.

Temples of the Vikings

Vikings constructed temples for their gods, goddesses, and deities, including Odin and Thor. Often, temples were used for rituals and sacrifices. Numerous large mounds found all over Scandinavia are believed to be sites of Old Norse temples. Also, scholars believe many of the temples were demolished and replaced by churches later. As of today, no Viking temples survive.

Viking Burials

Multiple archeological evidence points to the fact that the Vikings believed in the concept of an afterlife and equipped the dead accordingly. Dead bodies were buried along with many items, including jewelry. Burials were elaborate ceremonies that often included sacrifices as well. Human sacrifices of slaves were often performed because the Vikings believed the slaves would accompany the dead person in the afterlife.

The Decline of Norse Paganism Among the Vikings

When the Vikings started attacking and conquering the European coasts at the end of the 8th century, they were exposed to Christianity. Most of the Vikings that set out to conquer these regions settled in these parts of Europe, including Normandy, Ireland, and Britain. The settlers slowly started accepting and adopting the tenets of the new religion until, eventually, most of them converted to Christianity.

Soon, Christianity spread to Scandinavia too, and by the end of the 12th century, it was firmly established in the Viking strongholds of Sweden, Denmark, and Norway. With the acceptance and increasing popularity of Christianity, Norse Paganism began to decline. Some of the ideas were lost, while others were merged into the new religion.

Social-Classes of Viking-Society

Our social orders are always developing and numerous things have changed since the Viking age, and the vast majority of it to improve things. One of the significant things that have improved is the manner by which we see bondage. The Vikings did simply like most different social orders as of now in history have slaves, yet luckily, it is something that is nearly disposed of today.

Being a slave in the Viking age, was as you can envision not a generally excellent life. You were helpless before your proprietors, and they could do basically anything to you that they needed. A slave or as it is brought in Danish «træl» (Old Norse: þræll) had no individual flexibility, something that is even inferred in the word træl (Old English: thrall), which actually implies an unfree worker.

As per the old Norse adventures, it was the thralls (slaves) who were the top of the line of humanity. For you see, while it was Odin and his two siblings who made the initial two people from an elm tree and named them Ask and Embla.

It was the God Heimdall who made the four social classes when he went around Midgard (Middle-Earth) under the name Rig while wearing a camouflage. This story is told in the adventure 'The lay of Rig', however let me abridge the most significant pieces of this old Norse adventure.

The slaves were among the most significant wares exchanged by the Vikings. While it was principally from strikes and their campaigns to the Britsh Isles and in Eastern Europe that they got their slaves, they did likewise oppress their own sort in their nations of origin. For example, it was normal to see Danish slaves on Iceland, Swedish slaves in Denmark, and Norwegian slaves in Sweden.

The individuals inside the Viking society could likewise be rebuffed with servitude on the off chance that they had perpetrated a wrongdoing or were not able compensation an obligation. Wrongdoings that were regularly rebuffed with bondage, were violations like homicide and robbery.

CHAPTER 3

THE MOST IMPORTANT NORSE LEGENDS AND MYTHS

Ivar the Boneless

Ivar the Boneless is part legend and part historical character. You might remember that he and his brother Haldfan were the leaders of the great army that took Northumbria and Eastern Anglia by storm. Ivar also led attacks in Ireland and he is considered a founding father of the Viking rule in the kingdom of Dublin. Not much is recorded about him after the year 870, but it is presumed that he led attacks and ruled in the Islands of Man, Ireland, and other places around the Irish seas.

In Viking sagas, Ivar is the son of Ragnar Lothbroke, and his attack on Northumbria is an act of revenge against its king for killing his father. As for his peculiar nickname, its clear origin is unknown. Some historians believe that it stems from his fighting style and flexibility, which gave the illusion of him being "boneless," while others think it's a sly remark regarding his masculinity (alluding to him being impotent). An Irish annal notes the year 873 as the date of his death.

Thor's Journey to the Land of the Giants

Thor may have been a God associated with justice and righting a wrong, but he certainly was not peaceful. Indeed, wherever Thor went violence was sure to follow. Thor's mightiest challenge was to be opening a bag of food. Going on a journey with Loki and a servant, they came to Jotunheim, the land of the giants. They came across the giant Skrymir who suggested that he travel with them and transport their things for them. While camping, however, Skrymir fell into slumber and Thor was unable to open the sack with their provisions.

Thor attempted to awaken the giant by hitting him upon the head with Mjolnir, his hammer. Each time, Skrymir thought that strikes were just the fall of an acorn and he returned to his slumber. The giants left the next day and the travelers soon reached an enormous fortification. Inside the hall of the fortification, they met the King of the Giants who challenged them to best him in feats. Each of the three had to prove that he was better at a particular skill.

Loki was to prove that he was the swiftest eater in the world. He went up against the king's servant. The competitors were set at opposite ends of a trough upon which there were placed massive quantities of food. Loki ate along the trough toward the center, but when he reached this place, he saw that his adversary had not only eaten the food and the bones, but the trough itself.

Thjalfi, the human, was next. He was a fast runner, swift enough to outrun any giant. The king called a giant who was able to swiftly outrace the human. The boy wanted a rematch and only narrowly missed winning. He tried even a third time, but the giant ran even faster. The King of the Giants had to admit that he had never seen a human run as fast as Thjalfi.

It was now the turn of Thor to prove that he could best his competitor. Thor's test was to drain cold mead from a mighty drinking horn in only two gulps. Thor drained as much as he could from the horn in three gulps, but this resulted in little change in the level of mead in the horn. Next, Thor was to test his strength. Thor merely needs to raise the cat of the King of the Giants from the ground. But the cat was Thor's height and very heavy. The cat arched its back every time Thor tried to lift resulting in Thor only being able to raise a single paw.

Thor flew into a rage and challenged any of the giants in a hall to a wrestling match. The king summoned his old wet nurse. The woman looked weak and old, but Thor was unable to outwrestle her. The three travelers prepared to leave the hall in defeat, but before that, the king revealed that all in the hall was an illusion. Loki lost his competition because his opponent was a wildfire, which devours all. Thjalfi could not outwit his opponent because his opponent was thought itself, which can never be beaten by action. Thor could not defeat his opponent, which was old age, because age always catches up. The other competitions were illusions, too. The giant was so impressed by the performance of his guests that he swore never to allow them into his land again.

Sigurd

Sigurd is a legendary Norse hero who appears in many stories. Although different sources propose variations regarding his character and fate, he is usually portrayed as being strong, courageous, and successful in his endeavors. In earlier accounts, Sigurd is described as being of noble lineage, which might hint at a potential historical origin and his connection with an old Scandinavian ruler. In the Prose Edda, we find one of Sigurd's most famous legends—the slaying of the great dragon Fafnir. The saga speaks of how Sigur stabbed the beast and tasted its blood, gaining the ability to understand the language of the birds. This allows him to find out about Reginn's plan to murder him to acquire the dragon's treasure. Thus, Sigurd kills Reginn and keeps the gold for himself. He then marries the daughter of a king and helps his brother-in-law, Gunnar, ask for the valkyrie Brunhild's hand in marriage. But in doing so, he tricks the valkyrie by taking Gunnar's form to complete Brunhild's challenges. This whole plot ends up leading to Sigurd's demise when Brunhild takes her revenge for being tricked. In a different version, Gunnar kills Sigurd when he believes that the hero had slept with Brunhild.

In many stories of Sigurd's life, Brunhild is the one that inevitably gets him killed, in one way or another. But other legends see the courageous hero becoming a king of the Franks or learning the magic of the runes from the valkyrie Sigrdrifa (which is another one of Brunhild's names). Due to all the variations, we can say that Sigurd's tale is open-ended, leaving space for interpretations and choosing which version better suits our preferences.

Völsunga Saga

Volsung was the son of Rerir, born after his father's death from a long and lingering illness. He inherited the martial prowess of his ancestors and proved it by winning the hand of Hljod in marriage, taking her family, who were Jötnar, by surprise. Together, Volsung and Hljod raise a large family of eleven, of whom the eldest are the twins Sigmund and Signy.

When Signy is old enough to be married, she catches the eye of Siggeir, and they are soon wed—but at the wedding feast, Sigmund, Signy's twin brother, unwittingly offends Siggeir. In retaliation, Siggeir imprisons not just Sigmund but all of his and Signy's brothers. Siggeir also kills Volsung through treacherous means.

Sigmund and his brothers are placed in stocks out in the open, so that they may be devoured by wolves—but Signy defies her husband and finds a way for her twin brother to escape his captivity. He hides in a wood and Signy anonymously sends him assistance—and eventually, the two sons she bore to Siggeir with the intention that Sigmund should raise those sons and train them into warriors who will avenge Volsung. But the two boys fail Sigmund's tests of bravery and have themselves killed.

Signy then disguises herself and goes to Sigmund's lair and sleeps with him over the course of three nights before returning to the home of Siggeir. She becomes pregnant with Sigmund's son, whom she names Sinfiotli. She hides the fact of his parentage from her son himself as well as from her husband and her brother.

Being a "pure" descendant of Volsung, Sinfiotli is the ideal candidate to avenge his grandfather and uncles, and Sigmund consents to train him to become a powerful warrior. They waited for their chance to attack—and when Signy gives them the signal, they take Siggeir and all the rest of his children by surprise. The children are put to the sword while Siggeir watches, and then Sigmund and Sinfiotli shut Siggeir up in his house and set it on fire.

In perfect silence, Signy stands by and allows them to slaughter the children, and torch the house. And, as Siggeir dies, she speaks to Sigmund and Sinfiotli, telling them that they have succeeded in avenging the dead Volsung and his sons. Then she enters the burning house and dies at Siggeir's side.

Sigmund returns to the country of his father and rules there for many years. In his old age, he married a woman named Hjordis. But the suitor that she rejected in Sigmund's favor wages war against Sigmund, finally breaking his sword into shards and dealing him a mortal blow. As he lays dying, Sigmund asks Hjordis to safeguard the broken sword, and foretells that it will be reforged so that their unborn son might carry his father's weapon.

Eirik Bloodaxe

Eirik Bloodaxe is often portrayed as the stereotypical Viking fighter, with an overly Viking nickname. His accomplishments include being the king of Northumbria as well as the king of Norway. However, this last honor came to him in a rather dishonorable way. To become first in the line of succession he and his wife, Gunnhild, killed five of his brothers, earning Eirik his nickname "Bloodaxe" as well as the ire of his people. When Hakon the Good, another brother of his, rose to fight him for the throne, Eirik received no support whatsoever from the Norway people, and he chose to flee for his life. Not a very Viking-like action for him. Rumors at the time praised Eirik for his abilities as a fighter but condemned him for being dominated and too easily influenced by Gunnhild. So, despite his accomplishments, Eirik is not very close to the classical Viking hero.

The Mead of Poets

Mead was the drink of common people in Norse times though it had a special association with poets and skalds. Odin was said to drink only wine, and only men that Odin favored could partake of this drink, which must have been very rare in the Norse world as the climate was generally too frigid for the vine to grow.

The story of the Mead of Poets involves a certain Kvasir, who was a traveler and teacher of men. Kvasir was invited to visit two dwarfs called Fjalar and Galar. They asked permission to converse with Kvasir and soon killed him, draining his blood into two crocks and then making it into mead in a kettle. Odin and the other Aesir were told the lie that Kvasir had drowned. Following this, the dwarfs received a visit from a giant called Gilling along with his wife. The dwarfs went to fish with Gilling. The dwarfs eventually reached land while the vessel of Gilling struck an obstacle and the giant was drowned. His wife, hearing this, began to lament loudly for a time, and the dwarfs tiring of this dropped a stone on her head, killing her.

When the son of Gilling and his wife, the giant Suttung, heard about the death of his mother, he went to Fjalar and Galar and marooned them on a tempestuous rock. Fretting over this, the dwarfs offered to Suttung the mead that they had made. Suttung accepted this and peace was reached between them. But Odin, learning of this, began to covet the mead. He tricked the thralls of Suttung's brother Baugi into slaying themselves and then (in disguise under the assumed name Bolverk) offered to do the work of nine men. Odin, as Bolverk, accomplished this and convinced Baugi to help him secure the mead of Suttung. Suttung refused to give Odin the mead and Odin used trickery to obtain it: disguising himself as a snake in addition to other things. Once he had the mead, Odin turned into an eagle and flew to Asgard, pursued by Suttung. Odin spewed forth the mead that he had obtained in Valhalla, which was given to practitioners of the art of poetry, while the mead dropped by Suttung in his pursuit was allocated for poetasters.

Cnut the Great

Cnut the Great definitely beats Eirik when it comes to his Viking reputation. He was the son of a Danish king, Svein Forkbeard, who had managed to conquer England in 1013. But Svein's luck was tough, and he died shortly after asserting his claim over the lands. His oldest son, Harald, inherited the Danish throne, and poor Cnut received the mission to reinstate Viking control over England, which was already back in Anglo-Saxon hands. The young man rose to the challenge, and in 1016, he conquered England and married the last king's widow to cement his position. In the years to follow, Cnut also became king of Denmark (apparently through peaceful means) and the king of Norway (which he conquered in 1028). Thus, Cnut became the ruler of the largest North Sea empire of the Middle Ages.

CHAPTER 4

Myths Creations, the Main Gods and Goddess, Etc.

Creation Myth of Norse Mythology

According to Norse Paganism, before the start of time, there was a bottomless abyss referred to as Ginnungagap. This abyss separated the fiery land of Muspelheim and the icy lands of Niflheim. The two realms became powerful and strong and clashed against each other. The fire from Muspelheim thawed the ice in Niflheim and turned it into water drops, which held the potential for life.

The first living being, according to Norse Mythology, was Ymir. Ymir was a hermaphrodite giant who was created from the life-giving water drops. Ymir created children from his armpits as well as rubbed his two legs together, which gave rise to the jotnar, giant, and many other races. Although all the races were born of the same parent, a lot of animosities grew among races, and after a few generations, there was continuous discord among them.

Ymir's descendants were Odin, Vili, and Ve, who together killed Ymir. Then they used Ymir's bones, blood, teeth, eyelashes, hair, skull, and brain to create the Nordic world. The dome of Ymir's skull became the sky that arched over the earth. His blood became the waters of the lakes, rivers, and seas. His brain became clouds. His bones were transformed into hills and mountains, and his hair became trees.

The gods then created a protective fence out of Ymir's eyelashes to separate Jotunheimer, the giant's realm, from what was going to become the Midgard or the human realm. The gods then took over the job of overseeing this border they created to provide safety to the human world.

Norse gods are primarily divided into two categories, the Aesir and Vanir.

Norse mythology starts with how the cosmos, the universe, and everything in it, was made. It's basically everything that ever was or will be. Without a cosmos, you can't have anything else.

The Norse believed that at the very beginning of time, there were just three worlds:

- Muspelheim, made of fire
- Niflheim, made of ice
- Ginnungagap, a bottomless pit of darkness

Ginnungagap was in between Muspelheim and Niflheim. These two worlds of fire and ice shot out frost and flames, which would sometimes hit each other and fall into Ginnungagap. The drips of melted ice stuck together to make the giant, Ymir. Other giants split off from Ymir's body, the way cells in your body split apart to form new cells.

How the First Gods Were Born

Ymir and the giants weren't alone. The melted ice that made Ymir also made a cow, Audhumla, who ate a salt-lick that came from the ice that was still dripping. When she got to the bottom of the salt-lick, there was a person! This person was named Buri, the very first Aesir, which is a tribe of gods.

Buri had a son named Borr (sometimes spelled Bor), who married the daughter of one of the giants that came from Ymir. Borr and his wife, Bestla, were the parents of Odin. Since Borr was almost a god and Bestla was a giant, Odin was half-god and half-giant. This made him fit to be the chief of the Aesir tribe.

Odin also had two brothers, Vili and Ve. Together, the three of them made the rest of the world, including the sky, land, plants, oceans, and clouds.

Making a World

The story of how the world was made is a little dark. Most creation myths use the body of a god or some other type of creature to make the Earth. The Norse story of creation does the same thing.

Ymir was still around after Odin and his brothers were born, but he wasn't a nice guy. In fact, Ymir had turned so evil that Odin, Vili, and Ve had to kill him. Using Ymir's body, they made everything. His skull made the sky, his skin became soil and dirt, his hair turned into plants, and the oceans came from his blood.

After they made the world, the three gods decided it was time to fill it with a new race of creatures. Using two tree trunks, they made the first humans, Ask and Embla. The gods put humans in the "human world," known as Midgard. They also put up a fence around Midgard so the giants, who lived in Jotunheim, wouldn't be able to hurt the humans.

The creation story ends when humans are made. The great myths come after that! Before you learn any of these, though, you need to know about the other worlds besides Midgard, Jotunheim, Muspelheim, and Niflheim.

The Aesir Gods and Goddesses

Of the two clans of divinities in Norse folklore, the essential gathering were the Aesir. These were the most dominant divine beings, in spite of the fact that the Vanir weren›t actually weaklings. The Aesir divine beings and goddesses lived in Asgard, one of the nine domains of the universe. Asgard was something of a heavenly impression of Midgard, Earth, and spoke to request and structure in a disorganized universe. Asgard is situated on the sunniest part of Yggdrasil, the world tree that possesses the precise focal point of the universe in Norse folklore. The entirety of the domains are some place on this tree.

So who lived in Asgard? The pioneer of the Aesir divine beings was Odin, called the Allfather. In spite of being the head of Asgard, Odin is rarely home, and oftentimes meanders about the universe on singular missions for information and intelligence. Actually, he is depicted with one eye since legend claims he yielded the other to increase new wisdoms. Odin even hung him himself from the parts of the world tree and cut himself with a lance, scarcely enduring, so he could get familiar with the privileged insights of the amazing enchanted images of the runes.

Runes are the composed language of the Norse, which as indicated by custom spoke to ground-breaking enchanted powers. Odin had seen the ground-breaking ladies who inhabited the base of the world tree utilize the runes to impact the destiny of the universe, and he needed to pick up that astuteness. Through his a disregard for one's own needs, he picked up the support of the runes themselves, which told

Odin the best way to utilize their enchantment.

Thus, Odin has this double nature. He drives a clan of heavenly warriors, however distinguishes more with outsiders. He is a divine force of war, yet additionally of verse and intelligence. The entirety of this makes Odin one of the most mind boggling figures in Norse folklore.

Odin›s inestimable meal lobby, called Valhalla, was the Norse individuals› vision of the perfect eternity. Recognized people were chosen by Odin upon their demise to come to Valhalla, where they would eat and fight each other for excitement. This wasn›t actually similar to the Christianized perspective on paradise, be that as it may. The dead were not chosen to come to Valhalla since they were ethically commendable, but since Odin discovered them helpful. The warriors of Valhalla were a piece of a significant armed force Odin was aggregating in anticipation of Ragnarok, the last enormous fight between the divine beings and monsters.

Odin was the head of the Aesir, yet this clan was brimming with incredible gods. Generally celebrated, maybe, is Thor, divine force of thunder. The Norse individuals considered Thor to be the perfect warrior, the heavenly impression of what human warriors ought to endeavor to turn into. He was brave, enduring, and guarded Asgard from the goliaths. This is somewhat unexpected, in light of the fact that Thor›s heritage incorporates a few monsters, however he never waivers from his obligation. Thor likewise remains as a cherished memory to him for the people of Midgard, and frequently goes to their guide. The Norse individuals even called upon Thor to favor their weddings and shield the association from malevolent spirits.

The Vanir Gods and Goddesses

The Vanir are one of the two head clans of divinities highlighted in Norse folklore. (The other clan is the Aesir.) Among their positions are Freya, Freyr, Njord, and seemingly the early Germanic goddess Nerthus too. Their house is Vanaheim, one of the Nine Worlds held inside the parts of the world-tree Yggdrasil.

Shockingly, as fragmentary as the sources on pre-Christian Germanic religion are, we know alongside nothing about what the pre-Christian Germanic people groups thought of the Vanir as a gathering. «Vanir» is a seldom utilized word. Its importance is obscure. While there is a sprinkling of conceivable proof for the love of Freyr, Freyja, or potentially Njord outside of Scandinavia and Iceland, the title «Vanir» is never utilized regarding them. Some have even addressed whether the Scandinavians and Icelanders themselves thought of Freyja, Freyr, and Njord as having a place with a different tribe known as the «Vanir» before the compositions of the Christian student of history and writer Snorri Sturluson. The Vanir do appear to be to some degree more connected with human and environmental fruitfulness than the Aesir, however this is an ambiguous propensity, best case scenario, and surely not an outright differentiation; the Aesir god Thor, for instance, had an enormous task to carry out in the richness of the land and human culture also. Eventually, everything we can certainly say about the Vanir is that some late Norse scholarly sources depict them similar to a gathering faintly unmistakable from the Aesir, and the divine beings and goddesses to whom the title «Vanir» has been applied were among the most broadly and energetically worshiped of the pre-Christian Norse gods.

In Norse folklore, divine beings and goddesses generally have a place with one of two clans: the Aesir and the Vanir. All through a large portion of the Norse stories, gods from the two clans get along decently effectively, and it›s difficult to nail down firm qualifications between the two gatherings. In any case, sometime in the past that wasn›t the situation.

The Vanir goddess Freya was consistently the preeminent professional of the craft of seidr, the most frightfully amazing sort of enchantment. Like chronicled seidr specialists, she meandered from town to town handling her art for contract.

Under the name Heiðr ("Bright"), she in the long run came to Asgard, the home of the Aesir. The Aesir were very taken by her forces and passionately looked for her administrations. However, soon they understood that their estimations of respect, family dedication, and acquiescence to the law were being pushed aside by the egotistical wants they tried to satisfy with the witch's enchantment. Censuring Freya for their own deficiencies, the Aesir called her "Gullveig" ("Gold-insatiability") and endeavored to kill her. Multiple times they attempted to consume her, and multiple times she was reawakened from the remains.

Along these lines, the Aesir and Vanir came to detest and fear each other, and these threats emitted into war. The Aesir battled by the guidelines of plain battle, with weapons and beast power, while the Vanir utilized the subtler methods for enchantment. The war continued for quite a while, with the two sides picking up the high ground by turns.

In the long run the two clans of divinities got exhausted of battling and chose to call a détente. As was standard among the old Norse and other Germanic people groups, the different sides consented to pay tribute to one another by sending prisoners to live among the other clan. Freya, Freyr, and Njord of the Vanir went to the Aesir, and Hoenir (articulated generally «HIGH-neer») and Mimir went to the Vanir.

Njord and his youngsters appear to have lived pretty much in harmony in Asgard. Lamentably, the equivalent can't be said of Hoenir and Mimir in Vanaheim. The Vanir promptly observed that Hoenir was apparently ready to convey exceptionally insightful exhortation on any issue, yet they neglected to see this was just when he had Mimir in his organization. Hoenir was really a fairly moderate witted nitwit who was speechless when Mimir wasn't accessible to guide him. After Hoenir reacted to the Vanir's pleas with the unhelpful "Let others choose" one too often, the Vanir thought they had been cheated in the prisoner trade. They executed Mimir and sent the severed head back to Asgard, where the troubled Odin recited enchantment sonnets over the head and treated it in herbs. Subsequently safeguarded, Mimir's head kept on offering crucial guidance to Odin in the midst of hardship.

The two clans were as yet tired of battling a war that was so equally coordinated, in any case. As opposed to reestablishing their threats over this shocking misconception, every one of the Aesir and Vanir met up and spat into a cauldron. From their spit they made Kvasir, the most astute all things considered, as a method for promising supported harmony.

CHAPTER 5

THE ORIGIN OF KNOWLEDGE

The Day and the Night

A giant called Norfi lived in Jotunheim. He had a daughter whose name was Nótt (night), dark and brown like all the members of his lineage. She was given in marriage to a man named Naglfari. Their son was named Authr. Later, she was married to one named Annarr and their daughter was Jord (land). Finally, he was married to Dellingr and their son was Dagr (day). He was as bright as his father.

The Gods wanted to celebrate so they took Nótt and Dagr, gave them two steeds, so fast that they could complete a full circle of the Earth in twelve hours, and two beautiful wagons, and placed them in the sky to run around the earth every day. First, he rode Nótt with the horse named Hrímfaxi, "hoarfrost mane." Every morning, the foam from its bite dripped on the earth, creating the dew rains in the valleys. Dagr's horse was called Skinfaxi, "shining mane." Heaven and earth are illuminated by the splendor of his mane.

The Sun and the Moon

A man called Mundilfari had two children. They were so beautiful and shining that he called his son Máni and his daughter Sól, like the moon and the sun, and gave this to the man named Glenr.

The Gods, however, could not bear that a common mortal, guided by pride, would take possession of the names of their creations, so they kidnapped both and placed them in the sky.

They placed Sól to guide the chariot that carries the sun, built by the Gods to illuminate the world with a spark taken in the

Múspellheimr. The two horses were called Árvakr and Alsvithr. Under the shoulder blades of the steeds, the Gods placed two iron bellows to cool them during their run. Svalinn was the name of the shield that was placed before the sun. If it were taken from that place, the seas and mountains would flare-up. Máni was responsible for the movements of the moon, as well as for the growth and decline of its phases.

And there was still a reason why Sól and Máni ran in the sky without ever stopping, and it was that they were eternally chased by two wolves...

Every day, the impressive chariot driven by the beautiful Sól moved from east to west and was chased by the wolf Skoll, the "traitor," while Máni was chased by the wolf "Hati" ("hate" or "enemy"). Every month, it was said, Hati managed to bite the moon by removing a piece but each time the moon was able to move away and grow again.

The Helper of the Moon

Two boys were called Bil and Hjúki and were the sons of Vithfinnr. One evening, they were moving away from Byrgir's well, carrying on their shoulders the stick called Símul and the bucket called Saeg. Máni kidnapped them from the earth to help regulate the phases of the moon.

These two children can be seen on the lunar disk, together with their stick and their bucket.

The Lineage of the Wolves

An old female orc lived east of Midgard, in the iron tree forest, in Jarnividr. The old woman created giants in the form of wolves and raised them.

It was from this place that Skoll and Hati, sons of Hróthvitnir (Fenrir), came.

And it was also said that from this lineage came a very powerful wolf called Mánagarmr, "dog of the moon." He fed on the flesh of all the men who died and it would be him who, at the end of the world, would swallow the moon and smear the earth and sky with blood.

Summer and Winter

What is the difference between hot summers and cold winters? Everyone knows how to explain it. Svásuthr was called the giant father of Sumar, "summer." He lived a life so happy that, from him, whatever was pleasant took its name. The father of Vetr, "winter," instead, was a giant who some say was called Vindsvalr; he was the son of Vásathr. They were strict relatives and cold-tempered, and Vetr had their character.

The Sea, the Fire, and the Wind

The giants, who were very wise because their lineage went back to the origins of the world, had power over the elements of nature. It was said that an ancient giant called Fornjótr reigned over the icy lands of Finnland. From him descended a powerful and famous progeny: his sons, Aegir, Logi, and Kári.

- Aegir was the lord of the sea. His bride was named Rán. She had a net with which she gathered the drowned and transported them to her home. The nine daughters of

Hlér and Rán were the waves of the sea. They prepared the beer for which Irgir was rightly famous—so much so that it was in his room where the Gods gathered to drink and toast.

- Logi was the devouring fire lord. He was called Hálogi, "exalted flame," and he was the ruler of the province that took his name, the Hálogaland.
- Kári was the wind. His son Frosti, "cold" (also called Jǫkull), had power over cold and ice. The son of these was called Snær "snow." Snær also had three sons: Þorri "month of the fourth wind," the lord of the second half of winter, Fǫnn "sleet," and Mjǫll "fresh snow"; and a daughter, Drífa, "snowstorm."

Others, however, say that Logi and his sister Skjálf were the children of Frosti and that they avenged their father when he was killed by King Agni of the Ynglingar.

CHAPTER 6

The Royal Family, Asgardians, The Vanir, Deadly Offspring

The Aesir and Vanir

The Vanir – Historically, the Vanir, a tribe of farmers (worshipped later as ancient powerful gods), are believed to have come to Scandinavia and other parts of northern Europe about 5000 years ago. They brought the gift and power of agriculture, which is why they are considered farmer gods and goddesses. They came to this area after the flooding of the Black Sea.

Considering they were farmers, the Vanir gods are known for their connection to fertility. The important Vanir gods are Njord, Freya, and Freyr. Other deities include the Earth, Night, Day, Sun, and Moon. The day was believed to be the child of Night. Sun was female, and Moon was male.

The Aesir – Historically, the Aesir could have been male warriors who rode on horses and chariots. They are believed to have come from the East during the Indo-European invasions, which took place more than 1000 years after the entry of the Vanir. The Aesir warriors are believed to have wiped out most of the farmers or Vanirs (who were already living in Scandinavia); they retained the culture of the Vanirs and merged it with their own.

The most important Aesir gods were Odin, Frigg, Thor, and Tyr. According to Norse Paganism, half the warriors that die in battle are taken to Valhalla, a great hall in Asgard where Odin rules. The remaining slain warriors are taken to Folkvang (by Freya, the Vanir god), which is ruled by the Valkyries. The Vanirs and Aesirs are believed to have coexisted because the two groups, despite their antagonism, were required to combine their powers to prosper.

The Æsir lived in a land called Ásaheimr at the center of the world. In this distant land, on the top of mountains so high that they almost touched the sky, the gods raised the fortress of Asgard. It was here among splendid buildings and magnificent temples where they went to live with their families and their children. From that high and remote place, the Æsir established their dominion over the world, their rule over the elements, and the destiny of all beings.

While the Æsir settled in their heavenly fortresses, another lineage - the Vanir - chose to live in contact with the eternal cycles of the earth. Not much can be said of the Vanir. We do not know where they came from, what their lineage is, or who their rulers were. They lived in a remote land called Vanaheimr, whose location is uncertain, although some say it was west of Ásaheimr. Supernatural, mysterious, and powerful people, the Vanir were experts in magical practices, of which women, above all, were the authorities. Because of their knowledge and skills, they were able to see the future. The Vanir family was a society closed in on itself, jealous guardians of its characteristics and peculiarities. The practice of incest was common among them and it was not uncommon for sibling marriages to be celebrated.

In the past, says the volva, a term describing a North Germanic seeress, there was a war between the Æsir and the Vanir. This war ended with a reconciliation between the two divine lineages. Hostages were exchanged, so some of the Æsir went to live in Vanaheimr, while some of the powerful Vanir were welcomed in Asgard.

There are fourteen gods [Æsir] of divine lineage who rule the city of Asgard, and, likewise, there are fourteen goddesses [ásinjur], no less holy and powerful. The lord of Asgard is Odin, and these are the gods who govern the fortress: Thor, Baldr, Njǫrðr, Freyr, Týr, Bragi, Heimdallr, Höder, Vidarr, Váli, Ullr, and Forseti, as well as a fourteenth that must be added and that, is Loki. These are the goddesses: Frigg, Sága, Eir, Gefjun, Fulla, Freyja, Sjǫfn, Lofn, Vár, Vǫr, Syn, Hlín, Snotra, and Gná. Sól and Bil are also counted among the Goddesses, and we have already talked about them. Odin, the principal and eldest of the Æsir, is called Allfǫðr, "father of all," because it is from him that all the gods descend. Odin governs all things in the world and, although the other gods are also powerful, they serve him as children do their father. Frigg is his bride.

Many are the sons of Odin. The first is Thor, whom Odin fathered by joining with his daughter, Jǫrð. Full of strength, Thor surpasses all living creatures. The bride of Thor is Sif with the golden braids with whom he had a son, Móði, and a daughter, Þrúðr. Thor fathered another son, Magni, with the giantess Járnsaxa. Ullr, a great archer, and the skier is the son of Sif and her first husband and, therefore, is a stepson of Thor. Odin's second son, from Frigg, is Baldr. He is the best of the Æsir, handsome, wise, and kind. Everyone loves and respects him. His wife is Nanna, daughter of Nepr. Their son is Forseti, judge of the Gods. Baldr's brothers are the god Höder, who is blind, and the fast Hermóðr.

Odin is the father of many other gods. The giantess Gríðr gave birth to Vidarr the silent, the strongest of the Æsir after Thor. Princess Rindr made him the father of the brave Váli. The brave Týr is also the son of Odin, although others say he is, rather, the son of the giant Hymir.

Among the other gods, we count Bragi, supreme in eloquence, skilled in poetry, and the skaldic arts. His wife is Iðunn, the one who guards the apples that the gods must eat when they grow old to become young again. We spoke earlier of Heimdallr, Asgard's sentinel, who was raised at the beginning of time by nine mothers, all sisters. Finally, we must mention Loki, the deceiver's blacksmith, son of Fárbauti and Laufey. His work will be sadly known among the gods and men for as long as the world lasts.

We can add a few more on the other divine lineage of the Vanir. We do not know their origin, nor do we know who their rulers were. Of the Vanir we know just the names of those who, after the war that opposed the two divine lineages, abandoned the Vanaheimr and moved into Asgard as hostages, sharing with the Æsir the abode and the divine rank. These were Njǫrðr and his sons Freyr and Freyja. These two youth, according to the Vanir custom, Njǫrðr fathered with his sister. With the Æsir, however, a union of such close relatives was not permitted. Once in Asgard, Njǫrðr and his sons married in turn. The proud Skaði, daughter of the giant Þjazi, became the wife of Njǫrðr, although their union was not the happiest. Freyr married the beautiful Gerðr, daughter of the giant Gymir, for whose love, as we will see, he gave up his sword. Freyja married Odr, who was always far away on the road and much neglected her.

One day, a seductive woman arrived in Asgard: Gullveig, a sorceress skilled at sowing dissension amongst the Gods. She soon corrupted with cupidity the minds of the goddesses, the pillars of morals and honor. It was therefore decided to sentence the witch to death. Gullveig was part of the Vanir, who asked for her immediate return. Odin knew that not listening to this warning would lead to war but the witch's behavior was punished. The gods built a funeral pyre, restrained the witch, and then set her ablaze. The flames only consumed her body after three attempts. The fire gave the Vanir a pretext to attack the Æsir. Both factions fought furiously but the fate of the war remained in constant balance, bearing witness to mutual value. One day, using the strength of their magical arts, the Vanir managed to destroy the mighty walls of Asgard. Tired of a fratricidal war that had led to this ruin, the two families then signed a peace treaty and exchanged hostages. The Æsir sent Mimir and Hoenir to the Vanir, who handed over Njǫrðr, his son Freyr, and his daughter Freyja.

To seal their pact, the representatives of the Æsir and the Vanir then had a goatskin brought and spit in it. From this goatskin was born Kvasir the wisest creature in the universe and a living testimony of the divine agreements. The truce was immediately put to the test by the Vanir. They often asked the wise Hoenir for advice but he agreed to answer only if he could consult with Mimir. One day, tired of always having to wait for the two Æsir to consult each other before speaking, Vanir beheaded Mimir. Odin, full of contempt and pain, went to the realm of the Vanir, had the head of the god delivered to him, and returned to Asgard. He sprinkled the god's head with magical herbs, interrupting the decomposition process and preserving its wisdom. Since then, in times of need, Odin often converses with Mimir's head, asking it for advice on what to do.

CHAPTER 7

MYTHOLOGICAL CREATURES

Fenrir

Fenrir, the wolf who bit off Tyr's hand, is one of the scariest beasts in Norse mythology. Even the gods were afraid of him. Fenrir is Loki's son, which might seem weird since he's an animal. Gods could do that, though. Most of Loki's children were animals, not people.

Even when Fenrir was a baby wolf, the Aesir gods knew he would be very powerful. Since he was Loki's son, they were afraid he would be in trouble just like Loki. They raised Fenrir in Asgard so they could keep an eye on him. It's a good thing they did because he grew very fast. The gods realized that to control him, they would have to chain him up before he got too big. You probably remember what happened in the last chapter. Tyr put his hand in Fenrir's mouth so the gods could chain him up, and Fenrir bit Tyr's handoff. They tied Fenrir's chain to a boulder, and the gods put a sword in his mouth so he couldn't bite anyone else. Fenrir was so mad that he howled and howled, and all that howling made him drool. The drool formed a river that the Norse called "Expectation."

Nidhogg

Nidhogg is another serpent, but he lives under Yggdrasil. He eats the roots of the world tree which is very bad for the tree. The Norse believed he was a kind of giant who was trying to destroy the cosmos and everything in it. During Ragnarök, Nidhogg left his spot under Yggdrasil to help the giants.

Huginn and Muninn

Huginn and Muninn (from the Old Norse hugr, "thought," and munr, "mind" or "memory") are a pair of ravens that belong to the king of the Aesir, Odin. They fly throughout the nine realms, gathering information on all goings-on, and bring this news to him at the end of the day.

Odin is sometimes referred to as Hrafnagu, or the raven god, because of his relationship with ravens. The ravens, according to some interpretations, are personifications of themselves, representing their thoughts and memory rather than those of independent beings.

This is further supported by a stanza from the Poetic Edda, where he expresses worry that the ravens will one day no longer be able to return from his daily flight. Furthermore, he expresses greater worry for Muninn – that is, the loss of his mind.

Another reason for the ravens' association with Odin could be due to Odin's role as the god of war and death. Ravens are carrion birds, so they would be present during battles. They would benefit from the battle in a very real sense, and killing another was almost like giving the ravens a gift.

Another of Odin's names derived from this is Hrafnblóts Goði, which means "priest of the raven sacrifice" or "god of the raven sacrifice." After all, a warrior's death was a gift to Odin, because those who died in battle were transported to his realm of Valhalla, and it was common practice to sacrifice an enemy to the god before a battle.

Sleipnir

Sleipnir is Odin's horse. Sleipnir has eight legs and helps Odin get around to the different worlds of Yggdrasil. Sleipnir is another one of Loki's sons, but the gods aren't afraid of him. Out of all the horses in Asgard, Sleipnir is the best.

Norns

The Norns, despite their human appearance, are neither mortals nor Aesir. They aren't goddesses, either; their origins are unknown, though some sources claim they are giants. They are, however, more accurately described as personifications of the past, present, and future. They are, in a sense, unique beings who exist in their category.

The Norns, who appear to be three women, create and control the fate of all beings who inhabit the Norse cosmos. Even the gods are subject to their decisions, so they are the most powerful creatures in Norse mythology.

Elves

Elves are almost gods, but not exactly. They live in Alfheim, which is a beautiful land ruled by the Vanir god, Freyr.

ves are known for their beauty and magic powers. They can either heal humans or make them sick, and they like to do both. They aren't interested in anything that happens in the other nine worlds. Some elves marry humans, so their kids are half-elf and half-human. The human children of elves have magic powers that other humans don't have. Sometimes, when a human dies, he or she goes to Alfheim and becomes an elf instead of going to Hel or Valhalla.

Elves were kind of like perfect versions of humans to the Norse people, which is one reason they worshipped them.

Dwarves

The dwarves were known to be crafty beings that live in the realm of Midgard, hidden from humans in subterranean realms. The tales of dwarves go far back into mythology and creation, as they were known to be born of the flesh of the giant Ymir, along with the rest of their cosmos. They were molded by the Æsir into figures that resemble humans, but much shorter and gifted with intelligence and skill. These beings are artists in creating all sorts of things from jewelry to weapons and other intricate pieces. We see their skill in the creation of Thor's hammer Mjölnir crafted by the dwarves Brokkr and Eitri, as well as many other weapons in the gods' possession.

Valkyries

Valkyries, Odin's helper spirits, are women and female giants chosen to serve the king of the gods. Their name is derived from the Old Norse Valkyrja, which means "chooser of the slain."

Their primary task, as stated in their epithet, is to decide who lives and dies during battle. They are also tasked with selecting which half of the dead are taken to Odin's hall of Valhalla (the other half are taken to Fólkvangr, a field ruled over by the goddess Freyja). The warriors chosen by the Valkyries are transformed into Einherjar, who will fight alongside Odin during Ragnarök.

Ymir and Audhumbla

Ymir, the first giant, existed before the birth of any of the more well-known gods and goddesses. He was one of the first two creatures to emerge from Ginnungagap, the primordial void that existed even before the cosmos.

The frost giant was always ravenous. He was never satisfied, even though he consumed the milk of Audhumbla, the giant cow created alongside him. Audhumbla got her nourishment from a salt lick while Ymir drank from the cow. Buri, the first Aesir god, was discovered as she licked the salt.

While Ymir slept, other giants erupted from his body, including from his legs and his sweat. One of his descendants, Bestla, married Buri. Their grandchildren were Vili, Ve, and the king of the Aesir, Odin.

Surtr

Surtr, the giant, was born from the fires of the realm. He was a fire giant with a flaming sword who was stationed at Muspelheim's border to keep the realm safe from invasion. His name, which means "black" in English, is thought to be a reference to his charred and burning appearance.

He is destined to lead the other fire giants to war against the Aesir during Ragnarök when the world is destroyed and recreated, and most of the gods will perish with it. His fate is to battle Freyr, the god of fertility, sunshine, and rain. Surtr is destined to kill Freyr and be killed by him in turn.

Ratatoskr

Ratatoskr is a squirrel that runs up and down the roots of Yggdrasil, carrying messages between the eagle and Níðhǫggr. The Prose Edda states that he is gossiping and attempts to provoke hostility between the two rivals.

In some interpretations, the squirrel wants to destroy the world tree but lacks the strength to do so on his own. To this end, he manipulates the rivals into damaging the tree – Níðhǫggr chews the tree's roots to cause it to fall and kill the eagle while the eagle plucks branches from the tree to try and drop them on the dragon below.

In other representations, along with ferrying messages between the eagle and the dragon, Ratatoskr also carries messages between the gods.

Jörmungandr

Another of the children of Loki, Jörmungandr, is his child via the giantess Angrboða. A sea serpent, he is also given the names "Midgard Serpent" and "World Serpent," and is the sworn enemy of the thunder god, Thor.

Three major myths preserve Jörmungandr's rivalry with Thor:

In one story, the giant king Útgarða-Loki tricks Thor into attempting to lift Jörmungandr disguised as a cat. Thor succeeds in lifting one of its paws from the floor, after which Útgarða-Loki reveals his deception. Had Thor succeeded in lifting the cat from the floor completely, he would have changed the boundaries of the universe.

Jörmungandr, like his siblings Fenrir and Hel, was feared by Odin. The king of the gods took the three children from their parents when they were still young and separated them, tossing Jörmungandr into the ocean that surrounded Midgard.

In the time until Ragnarök, Jörmungandr encircles the world, holding his tail in his mouth. This image has resulted in Jörmungandr being linked with the Ouroboros, an image of a serpent or dragon eating its tail that is considered to symbolize the cycle of life, death, and rebirth.

Einherjar

The Einherjar, which translates to "those who fight alone" or "army of one," are the spirits of the dead warriors chosen by the Valkyries to live in Valhalla. They fight each other during the day. They are then healed every evening when the Valkyries feed them meat from the boar Saehrimnir and meat from the goat Heidrun.

According to legend, the Einherjar was destined to fight alongside Odin during Ragnarök and accompany him as he rode out to meet the wolf Fenrir. They will fight valiantly, but they, like their master, will ultimately perish in battle, along with the rest of the gods.

Draugr

The Draugr are undead creatures, often linked with the better-known zombies. They are also known as ugbúi ("barrow-dweller") and aptrganga ("again-walker"), especially in medieval literature.

Though the original meaning of the word "Draugr" is a ghost, these creatures (unlike true ghosts) are reanimated corpses and have corporeal bodies. They possess superhuman strength and can shapeshift, increasing their size at will and turning into animals, including seals. They carry with them the smell of decay.

They usually live in graves or palaces, guarding treasure that was buried with them. Aside from trespassers to their graves, they also target victims that had tormented them in life. They decimated livestock in the area when rising from the grave and frequently threatened the lives of local shepherds.

Kraken

The Kraken is mentioned for the first time in Norse mythology documents. They were believed to be giant sea monsters that looked like cephalopods (other members of the cephalopod family include squid and octopi). They lived off the coasts of Norway and Greenland, according to legend.

Kraken posed a particular danger to sailors, as they attacked ships with their multiple arms. The crew would then drown or be devoured by the creatures.

Trolls

Some tales from Sweden describe trolls as monstrous beings with many heads who can either live in the forest and mountains or caves. The first kind of trolls that live in the mountains are known to be large, aggressive, stupid, and slow beings, always getting outwitted by the hero in the story. Those that live in caves are shy and seen as shorter than humans with stumpy arms and legs but with a fair amount of intelligence. They use the environment around them to influence their power or protect themselves and hide. These creatures emerged into mythology from the idea of the giants (jötun) in their cosmology and realms, as the word troll in Old Norse is jätte.

Giants

These supernatural beings of the natural world have, from the beginning of time, been the arch-rivals of the Æsir and Vanir. They often warred, fought, cheated, and married each other. The jötun live in the icy realm of Jötunheim, which is closely connected to Midgard by mountain ranges and dense forests, while the fire giants live in Múspellsheimr, their realm of fire. They are the catalyst of the great ending in Ragnarök, setting fire to the tree Yggdrasil and ending everything in flame.

What one would think of giants in physique is their immense stature, but they were no bigger than an average human and resembled the humanoid beings of other realms. They represented the original nature of chaos and destruction in comparison to the gods representing life and order.

CHAPTER 8

NORSE TALES

Frithiof's Saga

King Beli of Sogn had two sons, Helgi and Halfdan, and a beautiful prized daughter named Ingeborg. Now King Beli had many friends, but his closest friend was his neighbor Thorstein, who lived across the fjord. Thorstein's own son, Frithiof, was a strong and bold man, known for his bravery and physical height.

Ingeborg's mother, unfortunately, passed away when they were young, and one of King Beli's goodmen, Hilding, took Ingeborg and her brothers, as well as young, strapping Frithiof under his wing as foster-father, so all the children had grown up together and become fast friends. Over the years, Frithiof found a deep and maddening love for Ingeborg that bloomed from childhood into their adult lives.

During a civil war, both King Beli and Frithiof's father, Thorstein, were killed on the battlefield, leaving the two brothers, Helgi and Halfdan, as brother-kings to rule over the kingdom. The brothers were particularly jealous of Frithiof and his incredible qualities of bravery and strength and were aware of his desire for their sister. In a petty and sly maneuver, the brothers transferred Ingeborg to a sacred dwelling far away called Baldrshagi, where intercourse and love relations were forbidden. This never deterred Frithiof's devotion to Ingeborg and still, he visited her and they continued to share their love.

This angered the brother-kings terribly, so they took action and sent Frithiof off to the Orkney Islands in Scotland in an excuse to put distance between him and their fair sister. While away to pay tribute as requested, the brothers decide to burn down Frithiof's house and marry Ingeborg off to the Norwegian

King Ring of Ringerike. Surely Ingeborg is mortified and obeys nonetheless, but her beloved Frithiof has no idea what has transpired.

Upon his return to Norway and finding the remains of his homestead and the absence of his love Ingeborg, he inquired with the brother-kings and discovered their treachery. In a rage, he burned down the sacred temple of Baldrshagi where Ingeborg once stayed, and took up his weapon and shield to sail to faraway lands as a Viking.

For three years he ventured, raided, and traded, gaining many riches and a grand reputation. When he returns home he decides to take up winter residence with King Ring so he may be closer to Ingeborg once more. Frithiof is a noble and kind man, so naturally, he becomes strong friends with the old king. Just before the king's death, Frithiof is named earl of King Ring's domain and care-taker of Ingeborg's first child. He then marries Ingeborg almost immediately, finally getting the love he craved all his life.

After the death of the old king, Frithiof takes up his revenge against the petty and untrustworthy brothers with who he grew up. He kills the eldest brother and makes the youngest a liege of his kingdom, bound to his service. And so the patient and valiant Frithiof now can rest and love in peace.

This inspiring and immortal Scandinavian tale of love, conquest, and revenge has many variations, but the moral is always the same. Ture love does not need to be rushed. Patience, courage, and honor will guide the true-hearted on their path to happiness.

Aegir's Brewpot

The sea Aegir came to Asgarth for the feast of Winter's Eve, and he was treated as an honored guest. In the evening when it was time for drinking, Odin had swords brought into the hall and they shone so brightly that no other lights were needed. Each of the gods sat in a high seat, and the walls were hung with painted shields. The gods served Aegir with beer out of Thor's own drinking bowls. But for all the splendors of Asgarth, Aegir told wonderful stories of his hall beneath the waves, of the great feasts he held there, and of the many men who sat around his benches. 'My hall is even bigger,' he said, 'than Thor's hall of Thunder Flash!'

It was then that Thor came back from Outgarth. He walked into Bright Home, and he saw Aegir with his green beard sitting in the seat of honor, drinking from his bowls.

'What is this etin doing at our feast?' said Thor. 'I have come back from Etinhome, where I did great deeds but was met with scorn and mockery. Logi Forniot's son was there in Outgarth, and he took part in their trickery. Yet his brother Aegir sits here boasting, and does nothing to prove himself.'

Odin said, 'Welcome, Thor. We miss you at our feasts. Tell us news of your long journey. What deeds have you done in Etinhome?'

'I drank and ate with the etins in Outgarth. I was stronger than them all, but still, I was made a laughing stock.'

'But tell us, Thor,' said Odin, 'did you not show your strength at fighting or wrestling when you were in Outgarth?'

'I did wrestle there, against Old Age herself, who throws everyone to the floor. I alone stood strong against her, but yet there was no winner.'

Aegir said, 'I think you'd do badly against Earth's Belt if you can't beat an old woman.'

'I lifted the Great Monster, that hideous serpent hateful to gods and men, from the floor of the sea. And yet I was tricked, so I could not overthrow it.'

'Midgard's Snake got the better of you,' said Aegir, 'and I don't think there are many who could overcome the Serpent of the Seas.'

'If we met again in a fair fight,' said Thor, 'then I'd finish him!'

'I think your powers are no match for the might of the deep,' said Aegir, 'and you'd not be so strong on the sea.'

'I drank so deep from Outgarth's horn, that I drained the sea half-dry!'

All Father said, 'My friends, our feast is almost done, and winter is nearly upon us. Who among us will feast us all for Yule at midwinter?'

Thor looked Aegir hard in the eye. He said, 'Aegir is drinking the beer of the gods. He boasts that his hall has longer benches and that he holds greater feasts. Let Aegir feast us for Yule this year and every year at midwinter!'

'You've already tasted too much of my beer,' said Aegir, 'when you drank so much of the sea. There's no pot big enough to make beer for you all. If you want to drink my beer again, you must get me a kettle to brew it in.'

No one was more worried about this than Thor.

'Where could we get such a kettle?' he asked.

Tyr said, 'My father Hymir in Etinhome has the biggest brew pot you could believe, an iron kettle a mile wide.'

'Those etins played tricks on me,' said Thor. 'We'll get them back if we think of a trick to get that kettle.'

So Thor dressed himself up as a young lad and gave himself the name of Warden. He took Tyr with him and set out for Hymir's house in Etinhome. His goat was still lame, so they went by foot. They traveled across Midgard without goats or wagon and reached the house at nightfall.

Tyr's grandmother opened the door to them. First one head peered around the door, then another, and then another, because Tyr's etin grandmother had plenty of heads—nine hundred in all!

Then Tyr's mother came out. Her name was Hroth and she was as lovely as the other was hideous. She greeted them kindly and brought them beer.

'You're very welcome here,' said Hroth, 'but hide yourselves up in the pots overhead, because my husband Hymir can often be unfriendly when he gets home.'

There were nine pots hanging from the roof beam of the house, and Tyr and Thor hid in the biggest. They waited there until long after dark when the etin Hymir came home from his hunting. The snow lay thick on his shoulders, and his beard tinkled with clattering icicles as he strode scowling into the hall.

His wife stepped up and said, 'Welcome home, Hymir. Cheer up, now! Your own son Tyr has come home to see you, and his friend Warden is with him.'

The etin stared angrily around the hall, looking for his unwelcome guests. He caught sight of the roof beam where the pots were hanging, and his stare was so hard that the beam split in two, and the pots came crashing to the floor. Eight were broken into pieces. Only one stayed whole, the great iron kettle where the gods had hidden.

Thor and Tyr stepped out, but Hymir's heart didn't jump for joy when he saw his two guests on the floor before him.

'I'll need to keep an eye on that lad, Warden,' the etin muttered. Then he said, 'Kill three of my bulls, to cook for our supper. I reckon we'll need plenty of meat tonight.'

The bulls were slaughtered and set to boil. When the meat was cooked, they sat down to dinner. Thor had soon munched his way through one of the bulls, so he helped himself to the next.

Hymir was watching Thor angrily and he said, 'Tomorrow, I think we'll find our own food, so there might be enough to go round.'

'That's a good idea,' said Thor. 'Let's go fishing together!' Hymir said, 'I can't see what use you'd be in the boat, so little and puny as you look. And you'll whine with cold if I go out as far and stay out as long as I usually do.'

'We've yet to see who'll be the first to whine for home,' said

Thor, 'and I say we should play a game. Whoever can prove he is stronger and bolder can take whatever he wants as his own, and I'll have that big brew pot we were sitting in.'

'This is child's play,' said the etin. 'A young lad like you could never beat an old etin like me, and I think I'll brew beer in my own kettle again just as before.'

The next morning, Hymir was up and dressed before dawn, and Thor wasn't far behind him. They set off down by the cliff, to where Hymir's fishing boat lay moored in the cove below.

Thor said, 'What'll we do for bait?'

'I've got my bait,' said Hymir. 'You get your own!' So Thor went into the field where Hymir's cattle were.

There was a great black bull there called Heaven Springer. Thor took it by the horns and twisted until the head came off. He took that down the cliff to Hymir's boat.

'I've got bait now too,' said Thor.

Hymir looked at the head of his best bull lying in the boat and frowned. 'Your handiwork today is no better than your table manners last night,' he said.

They took up the oars and started to row. The etin thought Warden's rowing was pretty strong, and it wasn't long before Hymir said, 'We can stop now. I have caught a lot of plaice and flounders and other flatfish here.'

'No,' said Thor. 'We'll row on out.'

After a while, Hymir said, 'We'll have to stop now, or we'll reach the deepest Ocean where the Great Monster lurks.'

But again Thor said, 'No. We'll row on out.'

He rowed on until Hymir said, 'Now we have reached the deepest Ocean, where the Midgard Serpent can get us.'

Then Thor brought his oars in and laid them down inside the boat. Hymir got to work chopping up bait with his long, sharp knife. He set the bait on his hooks and dropped his fishing lines overboard. It wasn't long before Hymir was hauling in whales on all his hooks, and throwing them down in the boat like flatfish.

Thor had a good stout rope for his fishing line, and he tied a big iron spike onto it. He took the head of the bull Heaven Springer, and set that onto the spike. Then he dropped it over the side of the boat, and let the rope slip through his hands as the bait sank down and down into the depths of the sea.

Down below at the bottom of the ocean, the Great Monster smelled blood in the water and turned his head to look. He saw the bull's head, he stretched his great mouth wide, and he bit. Then the iron spike stuck through the roof of the serpent's mouth, and he was hooked on the line.

Up above, Storm Rider felt the tug on the rope as the Great Monster bit, and he started to pull in his catch. Slowly, he hauled the Midgard Serpent up from the depths. But as he was pulling, the snake gave a sudden jerk with its neck and yanked on the rope, so that Thor's fists banged down hard on the side of the boat and he skinned his hands along the top strake.

Then Thor got angry, and he used all his god strength. He

pushed his feet down through the bottom of the boat, so he was standing on the bed of the ocean. Thor heaved on the rope, while Hymir sat trembling with fright as he stared at the sea washing in and out of his boat, and at Thor pulling the huge monster out of the deep.

Thor hauled that serpent up and up until at last, the head broke through the waves. And it's true to say that you've never seen a dreadful sight unless you were there and saw that monstrous skull coming out of the sea, or saw how Thor fixed his eyes on it, and how the serpent stared back at him spitting poison.

Thor brought his hammer up to strike, and he was just about to hurl it. But as the monster's head came up from the water, the color drained from Hymir's face and he went deathly white. He looked at the monster's foul head and at the waves surging into the boat, and he panicked.

Just as Thor was raising his hammer to strike, Hymir reached for his bait knife, leaned forward, and hacked through the rope.

Then the serpent's great head sank back beneath the water. Thor threw his hammer after it, and there was a screech from under the waves as it hit the monster's head. The whole earth echoed with the roar that rose from beneath the sea.

Some people say that Thor's hammer struck off the serpent's head and that the Great Monster died there, but many believe it is living still and that one day it will meet Thor again at the Doom of the Powers.

Hymir was silent and stony-faced as they rowed home.

'I rowed us out to the deepest ocean,' said Thor. 'I hooked the

Great Monster and there's no bigger fish than that, so I win the game!'

Then Hymir said, 'Well, I don't see that you've been much use today. I caught six whales for us to eat tonight, but you've caught nothing at all. It's true you can row well enough, but that won't win the pot. So, if you want to stay, you'll have to do your share of the work. Either you carry our catch back to the house, or else you can tie up the boat.'

Then Thor picked up the boat with the whales still in it and all the water that had washed over the decks. He carried it up the cliff face and threw it down at Hymir's door.

'Now do you see that I'm stronger than you?' he said. 'I win the game and the pot is mine.'

But Hymir said, 'The pot is still mine. It might be true that you've got some strength, but you won't be strong enough to win unless you can break my wineglass.'

Hymir's wineglass looked easy to break, so Thor threw it down hard on the floor. There was a hole in the floor where it landed, but the wineglass was unbroken.

Then he threw it against one of the hall pillars. The pillar snapped in two and a beam fell from the roof, but the glass was still unbroken. Storm Rider was reaching for his hammer when Tyr's mother whispered in his ear.

'You'll never break that glass,' she said, 'unless it hits the only thing that's stronger than it. Hymir's head is made of stone. Throw it against the old etin's head, and then it will smash into pieces.'

Thor jumped up on Hymir's knee and brought the cup down on his head. When the glass struck the etin's stone skull, it shattered into pieces and the pieces fell onto Hymir's knees.

The etin looked down at the broken shards which lay in his lap and he said, 'I know that I have lost a lot when I see the glass lying broken in my lap. I'll never again be able to say, "Beer, you are brewed!" The pot is yours if you can move it.'

Tyr said he'd try to move it, but no matter how hard he pushed, it wouldn't budge. Then Thor picked up the pot and put it on his head. He and Tyr set off for home, with the pot chains jangling around Thor's heels.

They hadn't reached the edge of Etinhome before they heard an army of etins coming after them. Thor had to stop and put the kettle down, to kill them all with his hammer. Then he picked up the pot again and carried it off to Aegir's hall.

The Story of Gerd and Freyr

Freyr, or Frey, was the son of Njord. He was very strong, brave, and handsome, even more so than his father. As one of the Vanir who came to the Aesir, he was another God associated with weather and fertility. He governed tillage. Men and women prayed to him for peace and prosperity. Under the special dominion of Freyr was the land of Alfheim and the good, or bright, elves.

Freyr was married to the daughter of a giant named Gymir. Her name was Gerd, and the story of their union is the subject of the present tale. One day, Freyr caught sight of Gerd while he was gazing at the wide world. He saw her strolling on her father's farm, and it seemed that she made the air and sea around her shine brighter. Freyr fell instantly in love, but he could not have her as she was a giantess. Out of his sadness, Freyr ceased eating and drinking. Njord was curious about what was wrong so he sent Skirnir, a servant, to learn what was wrong. Freyr confessed that he was in love with Gerd and asked Skirnir to ask for her hand on his behalf.

Skirnir only agreed to go on this errand if Freyr lent him his sword, which could strike on its own when it wished to. Skirnir used trickery to convince Gerd to meet with Freyr. They agreed to meet after the passage of nine nights, nights spent in painful longing in Freyr's case. It was said that Freyr's love for Gerd was a punishment for the God sitting upon Odin's throne on one occasion.

Niord's Children

When the Aesir and Vanir made peace, the Vanir gave the god Niord as a pledge of goodwill, and with him came his two children Frey and Freya. Niord lives at Boat Town, and his children grew up there.

Niord's daughter is Freya, and she is very skilled in magic. She is the loveliest of goddesses, and she is known as the Lady of the Vanir.

Her home is in Folk Field where she has a hall called Seat Roomy; its benches are filled with her handmaidens and with warriors who have fallen in battle. She has a beautiful bower there too, where she sleeps. When her door is shut, no one can get in unless she lets them.

Freya is married to the god Oth, but Oth wanders over the earth and Freya weeps for his return. She walks through the world searching for him and when she weeps, her tears fall to the ground as pure gold. Freya and Oth have two daughters, and their names are Jewel and Treasure.

Freya has a wagon drawn by two cats, and she has magic hawk skin. Whenever she puts on the hawk skin she takes the shape of a hawk, and she can fly wherever she wants across all worlds.

She also has a wonderful necklace called the Brising Necklace, which is finer and more beautiful than any other piece of jewelry. This necklace was made by four dwarfs called Dvalin, Alfrik, Berling, and Grer.

Freya first saw it when she was walking past a big stone. The door into the stone was open, and she saw the four dwarfs inside making the golden necklace. It was almost ready. Freya gazed at the necklace, and it was the most beautiful thing she had ever seen.

As soon as she saw the Brising Necklace, Freya wanted it for herself, so she asked the dwarfs if they would give it to her, but they would not. Then Freya said she would buy it, and she offered to give them vast stores of silver and gold. But the dwarfs only smiled and said, 'We do not need your gold. We have plenty to make trinkets like this one.'

Freya gazed at the necklace and she said, 'What do I have to do, to get it?'

The dwarfs gazed at Freya, and they said that they would take no payment for it unless she would spend a night with each of them, and they would not part with it for any other price.

The dwarfs were ugly, but the necklace was beautiful. The more Freya looked at the necklace, the more she felt it had to be hers. So she did as they asked, and that is how she won the Brising Necklace from the dwarfs.

But that necklace was stolen by Loki.

He saw that Freya had a splendid new necklace, and he could see how much she loved it. So he crept up to Freya's bower in the dead of night. Loki went all round the bower, and he could see no way in. But Loki can turn himself into whatever shape he wants, so he turned himself into a fly, and then he found a way in through a tiny gap under the roof.

Inside, the goddess lay sleeping on her bed, and Loki landed on the pillow beside her. She was wearing the beautiful Brising Necklace, but the clasp was fastened behind her neck. Still, in his fly shape, Loki stung her on the cheek, and she turned over in her sleep. Then he undid her necklace, opened up her bower doors, and walked out.

Loki took the necklace and ran off to the sea. He turned himself into a seal, and he swam until he came to the Singing Stone. He hid there with the necklace, beneath the waves by the Singing Stone.

The next morning, Freya woke to find her doors wide open and her necklace gone. But Heimdal, the Watchman of the Gods, who stands on Bifrost Bridge, looked out over the world and he saw where Loki had gone in the shape of a seal, and where he had hidden by the Singing Stone.

When Freya found her necklace was gone, Heimdal turned himself into another seal and swam after Loki. The two seals fought there, and they struggled with each other until Heimdal took the golden Brising Necklace.

He brought it back and gave it to Freya again.

Freya's brother is Frey. He had also come to live in Asgarth with his father Niord. The gods gave him Elfhome as a teething gift. That is where he has his hall, and he is known as the Lord of Elves.

One day, Frey sat on All Father's high seat of Lid Shelf, and from there he could see across all the upper worlds. To the north in Etinhome, he saw a beautiful building, and a lovely girl was going from the house out to her bower. When she raised her arms to let herself in, a light shone from her arms that spread over sea and sky and brightened all the worlds.

Frey thought she was the most beautiful girl he had ever set eyes on. Straightaway, he fell deeply in love with her.

When he stepped down from Lid Shelf, Frey was sad and sick at heart because he had lost sight of the girl. And when he got home he wouldn't speak. He didn't sleep and he didn't eat, and nobody dared talk to him. He looked troubled. He scarcely seemed to know where he was. He hardly heard when people spoke to him.

Frey could do nothing but think about the girl he'd seen in Etinhome. Her name was Gerd, and she was the daughter of the etin Gymir and his wife Aurboda.

Niord didn't know what was wrong with his son. He asked

Frey's servant Skirnir to help.

'You know him better than anyone,' he said, 'because you grew up side-by-side in one house together. If he'll tell anyone, it will be you. Find out who has made him so angry that he won't talk to anybody.'

'I don't think Frey will thank me for asking, but I'll do it for your sake,' said Skirnir.

So he went to Frey and said, 'What's troubling you, Frey? Why do you sit all alone by yourself? And why won't you talk to anyone?'

Frey said, 'Why should I tell you? How could you understand that the sunshine can light up the day, but not my heart?'

Skirnir said, 'It can't be so bad if you won't tell me when we grew up side-by-side in one house together.'

Then Frey told Skirnir what he had done and that he had seen Gerd, and he said he could never be happy until he had made her his wife.

'Now you must go and ask her to marry me,' he said, 'and you must bring her back with you, whether her father agrees or not. And I'll pay you well for this.'

'Then give me your horse that will go through the fire,' said Skirnir, 'and also your sword that will fight by itself.'

Frey said, 'I will give you anything if you will help me win her as my wife. And you must do whatever you have to so that she will marry me.'

Then Skirnir took Frey's sword and his horse Bloody Hoof, and away he rode to Etinhome. As he drew near to Gymir's farm, great flames flared up around the yard. There was a strong fence around it too, and the gates were guarded by snarling dogs. A shepherd was sitting on a mound nearby, and Skirnir said to him, 'How do I get past Gymir's dogs to see his daughter Gerd?'

The shepherd said, 'No one gets past those dogs to see Gerd. Turn back while you can! You will never speak with Gymir's wonderful daughter.'

But Skirnir rode on towards the farm. He rode through the flames on Bloody Hoof and leaped over the fence. Then he got off his horse, and let it graze in the yard.

Gerd heard the noise in the yard, and she asked her maid to bring Skirnir inside. 'Are you a god or an elf?' she asked him, 'and why have you ridden through fire to meet me?'

Skirnir said, 'I have come from the gods, to bring you back as a bride for Frey.'

Gerd said, 'I will not go to meet the gods or marry Frey at any man's bidding. My life is here, and here I will stay.'

'I have brought you Apples of Life from Mimir's Wood. They will be yours if you will marry Frey.'

'I will not take an apple for any man's sake.'

'I'll give you a ring of gold that Odin has owned.'

'I won't have the ring which Odin owned. I do not think I am short of gold.'

Skirnir said, 'Do you see this shining sword? I'll cut off your head unless you come!'

Gerd said, 'You can do as you want, but I won't come with you.'

Then Skirnir took out a knife and a piece of wood, and he started to write in runes on the wood.

'I have been to the living wood and brought back the branch of power. Now I carve these runes and this curse against you. Your wealth will wither and you will never be married. You will always want a man, and you will yearn for children. You'll sit out on the hillside wishing for death, howling with grief. Everything will stare at you. Odin will be angry with you, Frey will hate you. All this will be if you will not marry him. I have carved this curse in runes, but I can undo it.'

Then Gerd gave Skirnir a drink of mead and she said, 'I never thought that I would love the Vanir. You may tell Frey that I will meet him nine nights from now in a grove on the island called Barrey, and there we will be married.'

So that was the news that Skirnir took back to tell Frey. And when he brought him this news, Frey was standing outside his door waiting for him.

Then Frey said, 'Three nights are long, six nights are longer, how can I last for nine?' But nine nights later he went to the island of Barrey, and he found his happiness there with Gerd.

The Gifts of the Dvergar

One day, as a joke or out of malice, Loki cut Sif's hair. When Thor noticed, he seized Loki and would have smashed all his bones if Loki had not promised to immediately go to the Svartálfar and have a crown of gold forged by Sif.

This is the reason why, even today, poets talk about the gold "hair of Sif." Then went Loki from those dvergar, called Ívaldasynir, sons of Ívaldi, and they forged three wonderful treasures. The first was the golden hair, which would stick to the skin as soon as it was placed on Sif's head and which was able to grow like hair. The second was the Skíðblaðnir ship, whose sails, once unfurled, were immediately filled with a breeze that pushed the ship along any route one wanted to direct it. Furthermore, if desired, the ship could be folded like a tablecloth and placed in a bag. The third treasure was a spear, Gungnir, which always hit the target when it was launched.

Later, Loki, boasting of the three treasures forged by Ivaldi's sons, bet his head with a dvergr named Brokkr that his brother, Eitri, could not have built three objects of equal value.

Arriving in the workshop, Eitri threw a pigskin into the forge and ordered Brokkr to blow the bellows continuously until he ordered him to stop. Eitri had just left when an insect landed on Brokkr's hand, stinging it. However, following his brother's orders, Brokkr did not stop for a moment and continued to wind until Eitri came to pull a marvelous pig with golden bristles out of the forge.

Immediately afterward, Eitri put on the gold furnace and gave his brother the same task. Brokkr began to handle the bellows and did not stop even when the insect came to sting his neck painfully. He blew without pause until Eitri removed a wonderful gold ring from the furnace.

Finally, Eitri was introduced into the iron furnace and, once again, told Brokkr to blow with the bellows. The work would be completely useless, he said, if he stopped for even a moment. Brokkr set to work but, this time, the insect landed between his eyes and stung him so fiercely that blood ran down his face. Seeing nothing, Brokkr left the bellows and tried to catch the fly. Upon his arrival, Eitri was afraid that the work was ruined. He took a hammer from the forge and noticed, with disappointment, that the handle was too short.

However, he gave the objects to Brokkr and told him to go and dissolve the bet.

The Æsir sat on the seats of the council to judge which objects were most precious—whether those forged by Ívaldasynir or those brought by Brokkr.

Loki first presented the treasures commissioned from Ívaldasynir. He gave Sif the golden hair, Freyr the ship Skíðblaðnir, and Odin the Gungnir lance, illustrating the virtues of each object.

Then Brokkr presented his gifts. He gave Odin the Draupnir ring, saying that every nine nights there would be eight rings of equal weight. He gave the pig Gullinbursti to Freyr, explaining that he could run both in the air and in the water, at night or during the day, like any steed. Moreover, he added, no night was so deep, no place so dark, that it would not be illuminated by its golden bristles. Finally, he handed the hammer Mjölnir to Thor, explaining that with it, he could hit any opponent as hard as he wanted, without the hammer being damaged or broken. Moreover, he said, if he threw it at an enemy, he would never lose it. Mjölnir, in fact, had the virtue of returning to him, however far he could throw it. If desired, he could even shrink that hammer to such an extent that he could slip it into the collar of his shirt.

"The only flaw," he concluded, "is that the handle is a little short."

The Æsir, after reflecting, said that the hammer Mjölnir was the best of all the treasures, as it would allow them to defend themselves from the jotnar and the other giants. Thus, they established that Brokkr had won the bet.

Immediately, Loki offered to redeem his head. However, the dvergr replied that this was not in the pacts.

"Take me, then!" yelled Loki and fled. In fact, he wore a pair of shoes that allowed him to run even in the air and on the water. Brokkr asked Thor to capture him, and he brought back Loki without missing a beat.

Then Brokkr stepped forward, determined to cut off Loki's head. However, Loki retorted that he had committed only his head. The neck was not part of the agreement. Exasperated, the dwarf decided to sew his mouth. He grabbed a knife to pierce his lips but the blade couldn't cut into the meat. Then Brokkr summoned his brother Eitri's awl. Immediately, the instrument appeared in his hand. With that, he could drill holes in Loki's lips. Having done this, Brokkr sewed the mouth of the áss with a special hoop called Vartari.

Later, however, Loki removed the points.

CHAPTER 9

NORSE MAGIC

Magic was a major part of the Norse culture and encouraged several practitioners to perform magic tricks and rituals, some of which were necessary to bring prosperity to the Vikings. Even though we know little about Norse magic, several mentions about relevant practices and significant events provide an outline that is needed to understand magic in Norse paganism.

Magic was necessary for Norse mythology because the gods needed to use it to live and do their work. Odin needed magical power to wage war with his enemies, Thor would need it for his many tasks on earth, and Freya needed magic to keep herself alive as a goddess. They all had different needs and motives for magic.

Many people wonder why Norse mythology includes magic and into which function it falls. Magic is not simply present in the mythological world but can be found everywhere. Magic in Norse mythology plays a vital role in its culture and society. Many different types of magic exist within Norse mythology: there are the practical magics such as runes for writing or casting spells; natural magics such as the power of the runes; and spiritual magics like gods and goddesses possessing human beings to perform their will.

The Norse people had a very strong belief in magic, which played a significant role in their daily lives. They believed that if the gods were good and just and wished for the best for their people, magic would bring them back to life and continue life as usual. They believed that magic was necessary for this to happen. This belief, however, could lead to negative consequences.

The Norse people believed that if a person died and their body was burned in a fire, the gods would need more than just magic to bring them back from death. They required a sacrifice. The gods would then be unable to reach that person's soul when they died, and neither could they reunite with their ancestors. This is how the sacred fire was created.

Sacrifices were an essential part of the Norse religion. The Norse believed that the gods needed something from them to live and bring them back to life. So, the Norse sacrificed animals to their gods, hoping that it would bring them more power, good luck, or even happiness.

The sacrifices were typically animals such as sheep, cows, and horses. They were also known to sacrifice humans like Freya. The only sacrifice that was prohibited in the Norse religion was none other than human sacrifice. This would be considered taboo and completely unacceptable in any other religion.

As a result of the different ways magic is used and explained, there are also many kinds of magic. There is the "magic" necessary for survival, as the knowledge of medicine or farming in days before technology. Other magics play an essential role in society and culture, like religion and belief in fate or luck. Magic also plays a vital part in daily life and societies, such as legal systems, by allowing witnesses to identify criminals. Magic was essential to Norse culture because it was an integral part of everyday life.

Norse magic was practiced by specific cults and groups, some of which were hidden, whereas others attributed the practices to be their profession. Among several subgroups of magical practices, seidr, spa, galdr, and runic magic were the four main types of rituals performed by experts. While some of them had several similarities, others were solely practiced as an individual activity to reap maximum benefits.

Spá

This magical practice was also known as spae, and it was associated with the power of personal gnosis or intuition. This helped practitioners to determine ørlög, or the law of order, or how entities are supposed to behave. In order to determine whether or not certain things were in order, spa practitioners relied on their intuition. If not, they would offer concrete solutions or answers to help you achieve your goals. The term völva is interchangeably used with ørlög or Spa. In essence, völva refers to "Sybil" or "prophetess," which defines a witch or prophetess with her staff.

Some practitioners of spae magic also used their magic to access the stories of their ancestors, who could, in a way, predict their future. The women who practiced spae magic were highly respected because they could help the nobles make important decisions by predicting the future. They would play a significant role during war planning and provide insights to change certain motives in order to win. The Veleda was a famous prophetess who predicted the victory of her staff and the Batavi army who battled against the Romans. Based on the old Germanic customs, Veleda's powers were often compared to a god's, which made her superior and well-respected during that era.

Runic Magic

Runic magic involves the art of reading and deciphering "runes," or phonetic characters of ancient Norsemen. The characters were considered magical and relevant inscriptions conjured up curses as well as blessings. Those who learned the right way to read the runes held immense power. From changing one's misfortune to predicting their fate, the runes helped one transform their life. Some runic inscriptions solely existed to protect the rock or stone. According to the inscription, the person was warned about the misfortune that could befall on them if they dared to move the stone. This meant that the runes could either make or break one's future.

In most cases, the runic inscriptions that fell into the wrong hands would always cause damage and ruin the person's future. Therefore, handling and reading the runes was a skill. Some runes were also used to treat health issues or enhance one's health condition through inner healing. The existence of runes is not clearly specified in the Old Norse tales. However, the anecdotes do mention Odin hanging himself from Yggdrasil to learn more about the runes and discover the art of reading them. When he neared his death, he finally got hold of the runes and came back to life.

Households Magic

Numerous households had magicians, most of which were housewives. The ladies used distaffs and spindles to tell fortune, which is why spinning was considered significant in their households. The spinners with proficient skills were blessed with good fortune and luck, whereas the ones who mishandled or lost the ability to use a distaff were cursed with bad luck and suffered for the entire year. This is why most women took spinning extremely seriously and predetermined their family's luck. It is believed that the spinning goddesses took charge and visited each household to determine the quality of tools used by the housewives, after which their fate was decided and altered.

Such instances of the changing fates of children and families have been regularly mentioned in the Norse accounts. One such tale is named "Märchen of Sleeping Beauty," in which persistent spinning is used to alter a child's fate every now and then. This tale had a major impact on all housewives and inculcated the belief of piercing their fingers with a sharp object to draw blood during pregnancy, preferably in the seventh month. A wooden piece was also assembled and adorned with protective symbols to secure the pregnant women from evil spirits.

Furthermore, the ladies spun three linen threads with different shades of black, red, and white that were used for different purposes once the baby was born. While the black thread was burned with the wooden piece to ward off evil spirits and curses, the red thread was tied around the newborn's hand for protection. The white thread was tied to the baby's umbilical cord. These instances explain the significance of the act of spinning and protective threads in households. Women with magical powers or those who could chant powerful mantras used their ability to protect their household and newborns.

While the art of spinning was majorly used for noble causes, some even used it to harm others. The mothers of Old Norse households would often sense lingering danger around their children and used their weaving skills to make protective shirts for them. The sons who went to war were given magically woven Raven Banners that turned black on the battlefield when danger approached the warriors. These banners were mostly woven by the warriors' sisters and mothers to strengthen their protection. Shades of blue and red were prioritized among all colors due to their magical potency. Red was used in healing and medical applications.

From gods to humans, almost all souls in the Norse universe possessed the ability to acquire and practice magical skills. As previously stated, magic was prevalent in both genders but was more prominent in women. It was regarded as women's art and was inextricably linked to their livelihood. However, some men delved deeper and acquired magical powers who were later questioned about their manhood and shamed by society. Regardless, Norse magic and rituals have since been an intriguing topic that marks significant events in the Norse universe. It is believed that a few people still practice or are trying to acquire ancient Norse magical skills.

CHAPTER 10

RAGNAROK

Ragnarök was known to all. It was the inevitable end of all things both divine and mortal. The concept that war and destruction would take hold of the realms through fire was what every commoner, slave, and king believed. Therefore, one could say that their fate was set in stone.

Ragnarok is the catastrophic destruction of the universe and everything in it. The end of the world, so to speak. The word Ragnarok means "Fate of the Gods."

In Norse mythology, Ragnarök is the event that marks the end of time. The gods will fight with the giants in a battle in which both will die and the sky and the earth will burn after the final war between good and evil. There is nothing the gods can do to prevent it. Ragnarök is also the means by which the purified universe can begin a new cosmic cycle. It is, therefore, a cyclical end of the world, followed by a new creation, followed in turn by another Ragnarök, and so on, for all eternity. In other words, creation and destruction are like points at opposite ends of a circle; one cannot reach one without meeting the other.

The first sign that heralds Ragnarök is the death of Baldr. Killed by Loki and forced to remain in the realm of the dead, he obliges the gods to face the fact that they cannot escape their fate. Despite their divine character, they are, in fact, subject to the same fate as human beings. They, too, must die. This awareness, however, does not lead to resignation. Even if their actions are in vain against the destiny that awaits them, Odin and the other gods will still gather the most skilled warriors for the final battle against the giants.

The second sign is the end of civilization and order in the realm of men. Men will have forgotten their traditions, ignored kinship ties, caused fratricidal wars, and abandoned themselves to a profound nihilism. Depravation will remain the only ideal of mankind. Fathers will kill their own sons, while mothers will seduce them. Brothers will sleep with their sisters. Then a terrible winter known as Fimbulvetr will come, which will not give way to summer for three years. Torrential rains, wind, and dreadful snowfall will torment the globe, covering it with a thick and impenetrable blanket of frost.

The third and final signal is the disappearance of the sun, known as Sól, and the moon, known as Máni. The Skoll and Hati wolves, which have been chasing them since the beginning of time, will be able to reach and devour them, depriving the world of light and plunging the Earth into eternal darkness. At the same time, all the stars will burn and fall from the firmament, making sailors wander in the immensity of the oceans where every light has now disappeared.

The war will therefore begin.

Three roosters will announce the beginning of Ragnarök. One will warn the giants in Jotunheim, another the dead of Hel. The cock Víðópnir, from the top of Yggdrasil, will warn the gods. The great tree, which contains the Nine Worlds in its branches and roots, will tremble, shaking the universe with terrible earthquakes that will tear the Earth apart and destroy whole mountains.

At that point, all the chains will break. Loki and his son Fenrir, the great wolf, will free themselves from their long captivity and wander the world, sowing death and destruction. Even the serpent of the world, Jormungandr, son of Loki, so far confined to the ocean depths, will re-emerge from the waters, causing tidal waves, flooding valleys, submerging cities, and drowning thousands of defenseless men.

The infernal ship Naglfar, the vessel built with the nails of the condemned in the kingdom of the underworld, will leave the beach of the dead to transport the army of evil. Fenrir will advance with wide-open jaws. He will have become so huge and evil that his upper jaw will touch the sky while his lower jaw will rest on the earth, destroying everything he encounters. Jormungandr, his brother, the serpent of the world, will eventually take his side, spreading so much venom that he poisons the whole Earth.

Led by Surtr, the giant who sweeps the Earth with his huge flaming sword, the sinister inhabitants of Muspelheim will advance from the south, leaving behind them a hellscape of flames, and will reach Bifrọst, the rainbow bridge that leads to Asgard, which will collapse underneath their weight. Preparing for the final battle, the lords of terror will reach the plain of Vigrid, where they will meet their natural allies: Loki, who has escaped his imprisonment, along with his monstrous sons and all those who had been exiled and imprisoned in the dark recesses of Hel. All the evil of the universe will gather in that place.

At the same time, Heimdall, guardian of Asgard and Bifrọst, will leave Himinbjorg, his hall, and will summon the gods with his horn, without stopping. It is a signal that the gods know well, warning that the war has begun and that their destiny is calling them.

Odin, grim-faced but with fire in his eye, will wear his helmet and, holding his terrible spear, will mount Sleipnir and summon his champions, the indomitable warriors of Valhalla, whose loyalty and courage have not been affected, even by death. The newly assembled army, an immense expanse of swords and armor, will greet the father of the gods, who will advance, together with all his sons, to the battlefield that destiny has established for them. There is no fear in their eyes. They know that this is the war that will put an end to all the battles, in which all the heroes of the Norse pantheon will fight side by side against the giants and all the evil creatures present in the universe. Their only desire is to fight valiantly to the end.

Odin has no doubts. He immediately aims at the most terrible enemy, the ravenous Fenrir, who awaits him threateningly, showing him huge open jaws, a hell of sharp teeth. Thor, beside him, will be unable to help Odin because he will be attacked by Jormungandr. Thus, Fenrir will prevail over the father of the gods, who will be imprisoned between his jaws and devoured. Vidar, one of Odin's sons, blinded by anger, will face the beast and, pressing one foot on the lower jaw and grasping the upper jaw, will shatter the wolf's head, tearing it and avenging his father.

Freyr will fight against Surtr and will perish for giving his sword to his servant and messenger, Skirnir.

Thor, making his way with the deadly blows of his hammer between the ranks of the giants, will face his long-time enemy, Jormungandr, who is so big that he encircles the terrestrial globe. The strength of the god is incredible. After a long battle, he will succeed in smashing the head of the hated snake, which will vanish into the depths of the sea from which he appeared. However, weakened by the evil poison, after having taken the hammer and made nine steps, the God of Thunder will collapse to the ground, devoid of life. The same fate will befall Týr, engaged in an unequal struggle against the horrendous mastiff guarding Hel. At the end of his strength, Týr will be able to beat the mastiff to death before expiring.

The last duel will be between Heimdall and Loki, who will kill each other. Before dying, Heimdall will succeed in playing his horn for the last time, then will collapse on the fiery battlefield with the image of the end of the universe imprinted in his eyes. The guardian of the rainbow will be the last warrior to close his eyes forever that day.

Many gods will succumb and Surtr, by now the uncontested master of the field, will burn the Earth and make the Nine Worlds fall into a hell of flames, transforming the whole universe into a huge incandescent sphere and purifying it of all the evil committed that day. In the final reversal of the original process of creation, the Earth, now devastated by the most destructive war in the history of the universe, will sink into the boiling sea, slowly disappearing under the waves. Suddenly, there will be only darkness and the perfect silence of the empty before creation.

When Ragnarök begins, there will be a long and cold winter. The Earth will be covered in snow and ice just like Niflheim, and the sun will disappear. Humans will go hungry because no food will grow. Skoll and Hati, two wolves who have been trying to catch the sun and the moon since the beginning of time, will catch Sol and Mani. Skoll and Hati are. After they take these two lights, the stars will also disappear. There will be no more night sky or even a sky in the daytime. Everything will be pitch black.

Then, at last, Yggdrasil will shake. When Yggdrasil shakes, the mountains will fall, and the monsters that had been locked away from humans will be free. Fenrir will break his chains, and Jormungand will jump out of the ocean in the sky and fall to Earth.

When Fenrir and Jormungand are free, Loki will also be able to break out of his chains. Remember that Loki was locked up after Baldur died. Since he was chained up by the gods, Loki will betray them and command an army of giants. The giants want to destroy the gods and the cosmos. Ragnarök is when they get the chance to do it.

Why the Norse Believed in Ragnarök

Most stories in mythology teach a lesson. They talk about bravery, why lying is bad, and how to be a better person. Ragnarök is a very different story. It doesn't seem to mean anything. Everyone just dies and the world ends! Why would the Norse people believe in something so sad? Believe it or not, there's a reason why Ragnarök had to happen and why it was important to the Norse.

Life for the Norse and Vikings was hard. They had to fight and work all the time. Just staying alive was a tough thing to do. If you had to live as they did, what would you do? A lot of people might give up. The Norse never did, though.

The gods they believed in were brave, strong, and they didn't quit. Since these were the people the Norse looked up to, it makes sense that they would want to be like the gods. Stories like Ragnarök show that not giving up is important. Even though the gods knew they would all die in Ragnarök, they still fought. They faced their fate.

Since the gods handled death with courage, the Norse knew that they could, too. Life as a human can be scary. It was even scarier in the Viking Age. That's why the Norse came up with stories like Ragnarök. In real life, things end, and people die. They didn't hide this fact in myths. Instead, they let it inspire them to act like the heroes they imagined.

CHAPTER 11

CONCEPT OF TIME, COSMOLOGY

The ancient Nordic people did not see the cosmos as only the Earth surrounded by the heavens above and the underworld or hell below. According to Asatru, the cosmos was a complex system of multiple realms and planes, including the human realm. All these planes of creation were interconnected with each other.

Before the start of time, Muspelheim, the fiery realm of fire, which was in the south, moved north to meet Niflheim, the icy realm. They met at Ginnungagap or the yawning void, and their powers combined. Muspelheim and Niflheim's union brought forth two beings, Ymir (whom we have spoken about in an earlier chapter) and Audhumla, a primeval cow of gigantic proportions.

The primeval cow licked the ice and created a new being named Buri, and from Buri came Borr. Marriages among these early beings, as well as sexless reproduction by Ymir, resulted in multiple generations of beings until three godly beings, namely Odin, Villi, and Ve, killed Ymir and created the cosmos from his body parts. The cosmos created from Ymir's body parts consisted of the World Tree and the Nine Worlds. The World Tree, Yggdrasil, supported the Nine Worlds, who were separated by vast distances.

Some believe the theory that the universe was formed from the big bang. Others believe that God created the universe in six days, using the seventh day as rest. But what do the Norse believe?

It's difficult to say the exact creation of the universe considering much of what was written about Norse mythology was after Christianization took over Europe. For that reason, Norse mythology could be somewhat blended with Christian views. However, the creation of the Norse universe is based more on symbolism than actuality.

Yggdrasil is the tree in which all the worlds are connected. Without Yggdrasil, everything would cease to exist.

The creation of the world starts with an endless void called Ginnungagap. On one side was Niflheim, a frozen void, and on the other side was Muspelheim, a raging inferno. The frozen wasteland and the land of fire merged, forming the first giant, Ymir, and the cosmic cow, Audhumbla. Ymir grew from the cow's milk while the cow found sustenance in licking the salty edge of Ginnungagap.

From Ymir grew other beings who then procreated and spawned additional beings. Eventually, Odin and his brothers were formed. They killed the giant Ymir and his blood spewed so much that it formed the ocean, his skin formed dirt, his bones formed mountains, and his teeth formed rocks. His eyelashes were used to create a barrier between Midgard, the realm of man, and Jutenheim, the realm of giants. Niflheim was pushed underground while muspelheim was dispersed across the universe, creating stars and lighting the sky.

Time passed, and the warmth from the sky mixed with the rain that fell from the clouds that were created from Ymir's brain and produced life: plants, animals, and spirits roamed the world.

The brothers found an ash and elm tree when walking along the shore by the sea and used the trees to make the first man and woman, who they called Ask and Embla. Each brother gave them a gift that would be the very essence of humankind. Odin gifted them the breath of life and a soul. Hoenir gifted them mind, spirit, and will. Lodur gifted them blood and senses, or the ability to feel. From there, Ask and Embla populated the world.

Nine realms are existing in Norse cosmology. The center of their universe and what connects all the realms together is situated in Asgard, and it is known as Yggdrasil, the World Tree.

The story from the Völuspá poem describes the events that took place during the creation of all things.

Two great realms once existed: one of ice and one of fire. They were separated by a terrible void called the Ginnungagap. These realms were to be known as Niflheim and Muspelheim, in turn. From the eventual collision of these realms, the ice on Niflheim melted and revealed Ymir, the proto-giant, and a cow called Audhumla.

Now, Audhumla licked away at the ice and uncovered Búri, the forefather of the gods. Audhumla and Búri sired son Borr and daughter Bestla, who in turn sired the brother gods known as Odin, Vili, and Vé. The three brothers take it upon themselves to kill Ymir so that they may create the world of men from his remains. Flesh for the earth, skull for the sky, bones for mountains, and blood for sea. The World Tree emerged soon after the world's creation along with all the many beings and realms. Once it was all done, with the help of god Baldr, from the deep woods emerged the first two humans, named Ask and Embla, and they began populating the new realm.

The early Norse works of Eddic and Skaldic poetry assume the reader has knowledge of cosmology, and thus, not much explanation is given on location and specific characteristics. Although Snorri's work of the nine realms changed it slightly adding and removing realms to include Helheim, or Hel (the Underworld), there is an importance of understanding that in Scandinavia at the time these descriptions would probably not be recognized and be quite different. Theirs was a living dynamic faith, and our knowledge is but just the surface of a much larger iceberg.

Yggdrasil's trunk is said to rise at the very geographical center of the Norse spiritual cosmos. The rest of that cosmos, all of its Nine Worlds, grows around and from it and is connected via its roots and branches. So, the wellbeing and safety of the cosmos depend upon this great tree. If it should tremble, it signifies the coming destruction of the entire Norse universe.

The tree's name has an interesting series of components. "Yggr" means "terrible," as in fearsome. It is one of the varied names used to refer to the god Odin himself, indicating his great power. "Drasill" means "horse." The great tree's name, Yggdrasil's name, translates as the "Horse of Odin." It serves as a callback to the time when Odin sacrificed himself, spearing himself to a tree, to discover the runes and their meaning. Because the tree held his body upon it, that reference evolved in Norse poetry to imagine the powerful god as the rider upon a great horse, which became or was magically transformed into a tree.

In the literature of the Old Norse, Yggdrasil may be an ash tree or one that is so magnificent it does not exist on earth.

Whatever type of tree it was, it was very tall and mighty. In the Norse poem "Völuspá," Yggdrasil is called "the friend of the clear sky" and described as being so immense that its top rises above the clouds, its tallest crown has snow upon them, and wind visits the tree fiercely. Nobody has any idea of where its roots lie, only practitioners of magic can see the underworld and the full cosmos below it. The mighty gods are said to meet at the tree's base daily to confer.

Animals of all kinds are described as living in the tree's branches and among its roots. Around the tree's base, some snakes chew at its roots along with the great dragon Nidhogg or Niohoggr. "Nio" means "monster" and the monstrous dragon is said to be trapped by the tree's roots to prevent it from being unleashed upon the world.

On the tree's top branches, there is an eagle and a scurrying squirrel. The latter is called Drill-Tooth or Ratatoskr. He is said to move up and down Yggdrasil's trunk sharing insults from the dragon to the eagle and from the eagle to the dragon.

Nearby, four handsome stags graze on the leaves of the tree. These are called Dainn, Dvalinn, Duneyrr, and Durathror.

It is said that the tree suffers from the creatures living on it. Niohoggr is said to tear at the tree from below, and Ratatoskr to dig its claws into the great tree's bark. So, while these creatures' interactions may be viewed as somewhat humorous, the tree is explicitly identified as a mortal, being gradually nibbled at, suffering, and bearing its great pain because all of the cosmos depends on its ability to do so.

The arrangement of the roots beneath the mighty tree's trunk varies depending on which Old Norse poem you are reading. In some poems, Yggdrasil is described as having three main roots: one which is firmly planted in the human world of Midgard; one in the giant's world of Jotunheim; and one in the underworld of hell. However, in other accounts, there is only the Well of Urd, or fate, located beneath the tree's roots. And in a slightly more recent account, in the Prose Edda from Icelandic writer Snorri Sturluson, three wells are described as lying beneath the tree. In this writing, the Well of Urd is placed somewhat differently. This well resides not below the ground, but instead in the realm of Voluspá, in the sky. The root growing from this well bends up to reach it. In other words, the root is attached to the sky. It is there, in this exalted place, that the gods have their daily meetings. The second well is Hvergelmir, or the Roaring Cauldron, a great well that reaches into the Niflheim world, which is filled with ice. The dragon Nidhogg chews upon this root. The third one lies in the realm of the giants, and also belongs to the wise Mimir. Mimir was beheaded during the Aesir and Vanir war of the gods; Odin then carried Mimir's head around. It is said that the head still speaks and advises Odin and offers him counsel and knowledge.

While this interpretation of the tree came later than the others, some scholars believe that Snorri is drawing from older sources that have been lost. Mimir is connected to earlier writings about the great tree because Yggdrasil itself was sometimes called Mímameiðr or the Post of Mimir.

All nine different realms spread from the tree itself, or are positioned as layers from the roots of the tree downwards. Their mythology had various details about the worlds created and some written sources are less clear than the others. What were known to be the original nine realms are:

Muspelheim

Muspelheim is the realm of fire and home to the fire giants; ruled over by Surtr or the Black one. It is located to the south of Ginnungagap. In Norse mythology, fire giants like Surtr are considered to be as close to pure evil as possible. Muspelheim, along with Niflheim (the realm of ice), joined together to create the first being: Ymir. It is believed that sparks from this realm created comets, stars, and planets. According to some sources of Norse mythology, Muspelheim fire giants are expected to fight against the gods in Ragnarok.

Asgard

The Aesir gods and goddesses' realm is Asgard, and it is fortified by strong walls built by a frost giant and guarded by Heimdall. The plain of Idavoll lies right at the center of Asgard, and this is the place where the deities meet for important discussions. Two important halls in Asgard are Vingolf, where the goddesses meet, and Gladsheim, where the gods meet. Valhalla, or the hall of the slain, is another hall of importance in Asgard. The warriors killed in battle are guided to Valhalla by the Valkyries, where they are prepared for the Ragnarok.

Asgard is on a higher plane than Midgard. Human beings can reach Asgard in multiple ways, including • The Bifrost or Asbru, a rainbow bridge that connects Midgard to Asgard.

• Gjallerbru or the resounding bridge in Helheim.

- Myrkvid or the mirk wood between Muspelheim and Asgard.

- The rivers flowing around Asgard. Thor uses these rivers, as the bridges cannot withstand his weight.

Asgard is believed to symbolize the highest levels of consciousness.

Jotunheim

Jotunheim is the realm of the giants and the Jotnar. The giants create menacing problems for the people in Midgard and the gods in Asgard. A river called Irving separates Asgard and Jotunheim. The most important city in the realm of the giants is

Alfheim

Alfheim is the home of the bright or light elves and is believed to be a place of splendid beauty. The elves residing in Alfheim are also considered to be very beautiful. Very close to Asgard, Alfheim is full of meadows, forests, and beautiful islands amidst large seas. It is considered to be a happy, sunny place.

The Elven race residing in Alfheim is similar to human beings, although they are taller, fairer, and live longer than humans. Alfheim was a gift given to Freyr when he was an infant and got his first tooth. Alfheim is the domain of the ego and the place of intuition and instinctive powers.

Helheim

Helheim or Hel is the realm or abode of the dead. The Goddess

Hel or Hella rules over it, and it's the lowest realm of the Nine Worlds. Resting far beneath the Yggdrasil, it is close to Niflheim. Not all parts of Helheim are bad and dark. Some parts are like an afterlife paradise filled with light and happiness and some parts of it are dark and gloomy.

Also, Hel is not a place of punishment. Primarily, it is a place where the souls of the dead rest. It is filled with the ghostly specters of souls that have died ingloriously or lived a wicked life. Helheim is also the home of souls who have broken promises in their lives.

Helheim is reached through three portals, including • The Hell Way or Highway to Hell or Helvergr.

• Gjoll, a river of blood.

• Gnipahellier or Overhanging cave.

The gateway to Hel is called Hel's Gate (Helgrind) or Corpse Gate (Nagrind), which is guarded by Modgud, a giantess along with her giant hound, Garmr. The gates of hell are toward the south, away from Asgard, whose gates are to the north. Gjoll, the river of blood surrounding Hel, is freezing cold and also has knives floating on it.

The only way one can cross the river is by walking across a bridge that is guarded by a giantess. According to Norse Paganism beliefs, if a living person walked on the bridge, it would create noise so loud that it seemed as if a thousand men were trying to walk on it, but a dead person could walk across the bridge without a sound.

In the northern part of Hel, the mansion of the goddess Hel is located, which is called Evdinir or "misery." A wall called the "falling peril" or Fallanda Forad surrounds goddess Hel's palace. Below Hel's mansion is the place of punishment for the wicked called Kvalheim, and located here is a place made of ladders or snakes. The wicked people are sent here so that the poison of the snake drips on them.

Psychologically and philosophically speaking, Helheim refers to the collective unconscious aspects of the human mind. It also represents the human connection with nature and our ancestors.

Svartalfheim Svartalfheim is the realm of the black elves (the light elves live in Alfheim). Black or dark elves are known as Dokkalfar in Norse mythology. Like the trolls, the dark elves are connected with "Daves" or "dvergar." Some sources state that this realm can be accessed through certain caves in Midgard.

As defined by Norse Paganism, the cosmos is based around Yggdrasil and comprises the Nine Worlds that spread across the branches and roots of this magical tree.

Niflheim

Among all realms, Niflheim is also one of the oldest worlds and it's surrounded by ice, mist, and fog. It was probably the second realm in existence and was in Ginnungagap, somewhere in the northern part. The name Niflheim translates to "Mist World" or "Abode of Mist." The ice giants took over this realm and made it their home. It is believed that Ymir, the first giant, was born in Niflheim, the point where the creation story all began. Niflheim's freezing air and Muspelheim's hot air created a hollow dimension from which Ymir was born. A lot of giants significant to Norse mythology were fathered by Ymir. It was only after Odin and his siblings slaughtered Ymir that the cosmos was created, and the first humans were born.

Vanaheim

Just like the Aesir tribe of gods and goddesses was considered supreme, the Vanir gods were strong and wise but were not as popular and venerated. The Vanir gods lived in the Vanaheim realm that was equally blessed with knowledge and fertility. Vanaheim is barely mentioned in any Norse accounts, which is why we do not know much about this realm. This world was believed to be full of light and magic that provided utmost comfort to the Vanir gods. As previously mentioned, the Aesir and Vanir tribes entered into combat with each other and exchanged some gods to sign a truce.

The Poetic Edda mentions Vanaheim only briefly, which explains why we have so little information about this realm. The mention pops up in the Vafþrúðnismál poem, where Vafthruthnir, a wise Jotunn, plays a game of intellect with Odin who is disguised as Gagnradr. Odin asks Vafthruthnir about the sea god, Njord, and where he came from. He further confuses him by adding that the sea god was not one of the Aesir gods, but still had distinct powers. Njord was a well-respected god born in Vanaheim who possessed significant powers, Vafthruthnir responded. As part of a post-war armistice, he had to relocate to Asgard to dwell with the Aesir gods.

Midgard

The home of humans, Midgard, was located on earth. Life on Midgard began as Odin and his siblings, Vili and Ve, created two humans from trees after successfully killing Ymir. As mentioned in the previous chapter, one was a man named "Ask," created from an ash tree, and the other was a woman named "Embla," created from an elm tree. The gods blessed the first humans with speech, thought, wisdom, and clothes. While they could easily survive with these blessings, they were not enough to protect themselves from evil beings and giants.

This was when the gods decided to create Midgard, the home of the humans. They used Ymir's flesh to create the land, his teeth to make the cliffs, his blood to create the oceans, his brain to create the clouds, his bones to make the mountains, and the giant's hair to make the trees. Odin and his brothers used Ymir's entire body after rolling him in the middle of the ground to create a whole new realm for the humans. Later on, these humans worshipped the gods who created them to express their gratitude. The four cardinal points of Midgard shown on the compass were believed to be held and positioned by the four dwarves, Sudri, Nordri, Vestri, and Austri.

Niðavellir or Svartálfaheimr

Another realm that was home to a definite type of mythical Norse creature was Nidavellir. The Norse dwarves were believed to be master craftsmen and smiths who often worked with forges and in mines located underground. The Dwarves were known to be quite secretive and busy in their work and this realm was also located beneath Midgard, under the ground.

They could be found working in the caves or under the rocks as the realm was majorly built of stone. The name of the realm means "wane of the moon" or "new moon" in the Old Norse language.

The other name of the realm, Svartalfheim, translates to "Dark fields" as the realm was mostly dark and cold. The only light source came from the torches lit on the high walls and the forge fires that burned day and night. The fire created a lot of smoke in the realm that complemented its dark spirit. The talented craftsmen of this realm built several gifts for the Aesir gods, most of which are significant to Norse mythology, such as Thor's hammer, Mjolnir, and Odin's spear, Gungnir. Draupnir, the magical ring, was also believed to have been created by the dwarves of Nidavellir.

GLOSSARY

A

Aesir—Asgard's chief Gods

Andvari—A dwarf that Loki robbed of a magic ring and gold

Angerbotha/Angrbotha—a giantess who produced three feared monsters with Loki—Fenrir the wolf, Jormungand the serpent, and the Goddess Hel

Asgard/Asgarth—home of the Gods

Ask/Aske/Askr—the first man, created by Lothur, Hoenir, and Odin

Asynjur—the Asgard Goddesses

Atli—Gudrun's second husband, who invited Higni and Gunnar to his court, where Gudrun slew them both and then slayed Gudrun

Audhumia/Audhumbla—the cow that Buri created by licking an ice cliff and that nourished Ymir

B

Balder/Baldr/Baldur—the God of spring, light, peace, and joy, Odin's son. Loki instigated his slaying at the hands of Hoth

Bifrost—the rainbow bridge between Asgard and Midgard

Bragi/Brage—the God of poetry and Ithunn's husband

Branstock—the great oak in the Volsungs hall, where Gram was thrust by Odin and could only be drawn forth by Sigmund

Brynhild—Valkyrie. Sigurd awakened Brynhild from a magic sleep. Married to Gunnar, responsible for Sigurd's death, took her own life and burned with Sigurd on the pyre

Bur/Bor—Bur's son and father to Lothur, Hoenir, and Odin

Buri/Bori—Bur's father and progenitor of Gods

E

Embla—created by Lothur, Hoenir, and Odin, Embla was the first woman

F

Fafnir—Rodmar's son. Fafnir slew Rodmar for gold in an otter's skin, guarded the gold in a dragon's skin, and was eventually slain by Vitharr

Fenrir—a terrible wolf born of Loki and Angrbotha who swallowed Odin at Ragnarök and was also slain by Vitharr

Forseti—Baldr's son

Frey/Freyr—the God of crops and fertility, Njorth's son, and originally of Vanir

Freya/Freyja—the Goddess of beauty and love, Frey's sister and originally of Vanir

Frigg/Frigga—Odin's wife and the Goddess of the sky

G

Garm—Hel's watchdog, slays Tyr at Ragnarök and is slain by Tyr

Gimle—Second to Ragnarök as the home of the blessed

Giuki—The king of Niebelungs, and father to Gudrun, Guttorm, Hogni and Gunnar

Glathsehim/Gladsheim—Asgard's Hall of the Gods

Gram—Sigmund's sword. Regin rewelded it, and Sigurd used it to slay Fafnir

Greyfell—Sigmund's horse, one of Sleipnir's descendants

Grimhild—Gudrun's mother, responsible for giving Sigurd the magic potion to forget Brynhild

Gudrun—Giuki's daughter, Sigurd's wife, and Jonakr and Atli's late wife

Gunnar—Giuki's son. Sigurd pretended to be Gunnar to win Brynhild. Gunnar was slain at the Hall of Atli

Guttorm—Giuki's son. At Brynhild's request, he slew Sigurd

H

Heimdall/Heimdallr—Asgard's guardian

Hel—The Goddess of the dead and the Queen of the Underworld, also Loki's daughter

Hiordis—Sigmund's wife and Sigurd's mother

Hoenir—Bur's son and one of Embla and Ask's creators

Hogni—Giuki's son, slain at Atli

Hoth/Hoder/Hodur—the blind God of the darkness and the night, slew Baldr at Loki's instigation

I

Ithunn/Ithun/Iduna—Bragi's wife and keeper of the Golden Apples of Youth

J

Jonakr—Gudrun's third husband

Jormunrek—Swanhild's slayer, slain by Gudrun's sons

Jotunnheim/Jotunheim—the giants' abode

L

Lif and Lifthrasir—after Ragnarök, these were the first man and woman

Loki—the God of mischief and evil, instigated Baldr's death

Lothur/Lodur—one of Ask and Embla's creators

M

Midgard—the Earth, mankind's abode

Midgard Serpent—Loki's offspring, a terrible sea monster who slays Thor at Ragnarök and is slain by Thor

Mimir—a giant, knower of the future and past, and guardian of the well at the root of Yggdrasil in Jotunheim

Mjölnir—Thor's magic hammer

N

Naglfar—the ship the giants used to attack Asgard at Ragnarök, built from dead men's nails

Nanna—Baldr's wife

Nibelungs—those who dwelled in the Northern Kingdom that Giuki ruled

Niflheim/Nifelheim—Hel's abode, the outer region of darkness and cold

Njorth—Frey and Freya's father, originally of Vanir

Norns—the Demi goddesses of fate—Urth (the past), Verdandi (the present), and Skuld (the future)

O

Odin/Othin—Aesir's head and creator of the world with Ve and Vili. Woden/Wodan's equivalent

Otter—Rodmar's son, slain by Loki. His skin was filled with gold from Andvari to make Rodmar happy

R

Ragnarok—the final destruction of the world after a battle between the giants and the gods. A few minor gods survive, and the world will be repopulated by Lif and Lifthrasir

Regin—Rodmar's son, a blacksmith and Sigurd's foster father

Rerir—Sigi's son and King of Huns

Rodmar—Regin, Fafnir and Otter's father, responsible for demanding gold be used to fill Otter's skin. Slain after he caught Fenrir stealing the gold

S

Sif—Thor's wife

Siggeir—the King of Goths and Signy's husband. Siggeir and his sons were responsible for slaying Volsung and his sons (not Sigmund.) He was slain by Sinflotli and Sigmund

Sigi—Odin's son and King of Huns

Sigmund—Volsung's son, Signy's brother, and Hiordis's husband

Signy—Volsung's daughter, Sigmund's sister, Siggeir's wife

Sigurd—Sigmund and Hiordis's son, Brynhild, awakened him from a magical sleep. Married to Gudrun and slain at Brynhild's instigation by Guttorm

Sigyn—Loki's wife

Sinflotli—Signy and Sigmund's son

Skuld—a Norn

Sleipnir/Sleipner—Odin's 8-legged horse

Surt/Surtr—a fire demon who slew Frey at Ragnarök

Svartalfaheim—the dwarves abode

Swanhild—Sigurd and Gudrun's daughter, Jormunrek slew her

T

Thor—Odin's oldest son, the God of Thunder

Tyr—Odin's son, the God of War

U

Ull/Ullr—Sif's son, Thor's stepson

Urth—a Norn

V

Valhalla/Valhall—one of Asgard's great halls where Odin

received the souls of heroics slain in battle

Vali—Odin's son and a survivor of Ragnarök

Valkyries—virgins, Odin's messengers responsible for choosing those who would die in battle and take them to Valhalla. There are thought to be nine Valkyries

Vanir—one of the earlier races of Gods, three of the survivors are associated with Aesir—Frey, Freya, and Njorth

Ve—Odin's brother and one of the world's creators

Verthandi—a Norn

Vili—Odin's brother, one of the world's creators

Vingolf—The Goddesses abode in Asgard

Vitharr/Vithar—Odin's son, a Ragnarök survivor

Volsung's—Odin's descendent and Signy's father

Y

Yggdrasill—the giant ash tree that came from Ymir's body, its roots stretched to Niffheim, Jotunnheim, and Asgard

Ymir/Ymer—an ancient frost giant slain by Ve, Vili, and Odin. His body created the world and Yggdrasill

Printed in Great Britain
by Amazon

82909579R00086